The Complete MacBook for Seniors Guide

Easy and Practical Tips for Beginners

The Digital Grandson's Guide to Tech

DIGITAL GRANDSON PRESS

The Complete MacBook for Seniors Guide: Easy and Practical Tips for Beginners

Publisher's Note
The information provided in this book is designed to be a helpful and informative guide for beginners learning to use technology, specifically the MacBook. While the publisher and author have made every effort to ensure the information is accurate at the time of publication, technology is constantly evolving. Therefore, we cannot guarantee the completeness, accuracy, or timeliness of the contents.

Trademarks
Apple, MacBook, macOS, Siri, and FaceTime are trademarks of Apple Inc., registered in the U.S. and other countries. All other trademarks are the property of their respective owners. The use of these trademarks is not intended to imply any affiliation with or endorsement by Apple Inc.

ISBN: 9798346662082
ASIN (eBook): B0CX4YVFCY

First Edition

Disclaimers
This book is intended for educational purposes only. The publisher and the author make no representations or warranties with respect to the accuracy, applicability, fitness, or completeness of the contents of this book. The information contained in this book is strictly for educational purposes. Readers are advised to use their best judgment and consult with a professional for any specific concerns.

Portions of this book were created using AI tools, specifically to assist with drafting and editing. All content has been reviewed, edited, and approved by the author to ensure accuracy, clarity, and quality. The use of AI is intended to enhance the writing process and provide clear, easy-to-follow instructions.

CONTENTS

WELCOME TO YOUR MACBOOK ADVENTURE!

YOUR DIGITAL GRANDSON IS HERE TO HELP

Welcome to your new MacBook adventure! Think of this guide as your trusty companion—your digital grandson—here to help you settle into your new technology without stress or frustration. Learning something new can feel challenging, but you're not alone. I'll be here every step of the way, cheering you on. You've got this!

Over the years, I've helped many older adults get started with new technology, and I've noticed a common pattern. Out comes the pen and paper as they try to jot down every step. Before long, frustration builds because this supposedly "intuitive" technology can feel anything but intuitive. If that sounds familiar, don't worry—you're in the right place. This guide is for you, providing clear, simple instructions without the pressure of figuring everything out on your own.

We'll start with the basics of using your MacBook: how to set it up, send emails, browse the web, and stay in touch with loved ones. No prior experience is needed—just a willingness to learn. Step by step, we'll tackle each topic, and before you know it, you'll be a MacBook Pro! (That's a computer pun. Get ready for a few of those along the way.)

If technology has ever left you feeling perplexed or stuck, fear not. I'll break things down into manageable pieces, and we'll approach every topic clearly and systematically. Along the way, we'll celebrate your progress—because every small step forward is an accomplishment worth recognizing.

Think of this like the first time you learned to drive. There was a lot to figure out at first—how to use the brakes, steer, and start the car—but eventually, it became second nature. Learning your MacBook is the same way. We'll begin by finding the "ignition," and soon enough, you'll be cruising through new possibilities from the comfort of your own home.

What Will This Guide Cover?

Learning new technology can be frustrating—we've all yelled at a printer or struggled to remember yet another password. You're not alone! My goal is to make this process enjoyable and empowering.

Each chapter focuses on a specific aspect of using your MacBook. We'll begin by setting it up, then move on to understanding the interface, using essential apps, and staying safe online. You'll also find tips and tricks, like keyboard shortcuts and how to adjust your preferences. I've even included a chapter on troubleshooting common issues so you'll know exactly what to do when something goes wrong.

The best part? You don't have to go through this guide in order! Feel free to skip sections you're already comfortable with and dive into the topics that interest you most. The book is always here if you want to come back later. That said, we recommend starting with Parts 1 and 2 to build a solid foundation for the rest of your MacBook journey.

By the time you've finished this guide, you won't just know how to use your MacBook—you'll also have the confidence to explore and learn new things on your own. Learning is a journey, and it's okay to go at your own pace. Every bit of knowledge you gain is a success worth celebrating.

Don't Be Afraid of Mistakes

Worried about making mistakes? That's completely normal! Learning anything new requires making a few missteps along the way. Trust me, I've made plenty myself! Think of it like learning to ride a bike. You might wobble and fall at first, but each attempt gets you closer to success.

The good news? Your MacBook is designed to be forgiving. It's pretty hard to break, and there's almost always a way to fix things. So take a deep breath, experiment, and don't be afraid to press a few buttons. If something doesn't go as planned, we'll figure it out together.

Staying in Touch and Enjoying Yourself

Your MacBook is more than just a computer—it's a gateway to staying connected with loved ones and enjoying your favorite activities. Whether you're FaceTiming your grandkids, sharing garden photos with a friend, reading a new book, or listening to your favorite music, your MacBook has you covered.

For example, FaceTime is Apple's video calling app that lets you have virtual face-to-face chats with friends and family, no matter where they are. It's like opening a window to your loved ones' world. And then there's Siri, Apple's friendly assistant. Imagine having your own personal helper to answer questions, remind you of tasks, or even tell you a joke. Siri is always ready to lend a hand and lighten your load.

Use the Glossary

Learning new technology often means encountering unfamiliar terms, and that's where the glossary at the back of this guide comes in. Whenever you come across a term that's new to you, simply flip to the glossary for a clear explanation. Think of it as your trusty translation guide to the language of technology.

A Note on Technology's Ever-Changing Nature

Before we dive into the amazing things your MacBook can do, let's acknowledge one important truth: technology evolves. Fast. That means some features or menu options might look slightly different from what's described in this book. Don't worry—you're not doing anything wrong, and your MacBook isn't broken. It's just the nature of technology, always changing and improving.

I've done my best to ensure this guide is as accurate and up to date as possible. However, if you find that something doesn't match what you see on your screen, visit **The Digital Grandson's Guide to Tech** website at www.thedigitalgrandson.com for updates, new tips, and answers to your questions. You can also contact me directly if you need help with something specific. Your feedback not only helps me improve the guide but also ensures others benefit from your discoveries.

Learning to navigate technology means adjusting to changes along the way, but here's the good news: I'll be with you every step of the journey. Together, we'll keep you up to date on the latest and greatest ways to make the most of your MacBook.

Let's Get Started

Your MacBook is filled with possibilities, and you're about to unlock them one step at a time. Progress, not perfection, is the goal. Every small step you take is a victory, and I'm here to celebrate each one with you.

So grab your MacBook, get comfortable, and let's get started. You've already taken the hardest step by opening this book, and I couldn't be more proud. Let's do this together!

Getting Started with Your MacBook

DIGITAL GRANDSON PRESS

UNBOXING YOUR MACBOOK

LET'S GET STARTED, ONE STEP AT A TIME

Congratulations! You're about to embark on an exciting adventure with your MacBook. Think of this moment like opening a gift that's full of possibilities—exciting, maybe a little overwhelming, but ultimately rewarding. Don't worry; I'm here to guide you every step of the way, like your tech-savvy grandson, making sure you feel comfortable and confident as we go.

Let's start with the basics: unboxing your MacBook and getting it ready to go. Take your time—there's no rush. By the end of this chapter, your MacBook will be powered up and ready for its first steps with you at the helm.

What's in the Box?

When you open the box, you'll find:

- **The MacBook itself:** This is the star of the show—your sleek, dependable companion.

- **A power adapter:** Think of this as your MacBook's lifeline for staying charged.

- **A charging cable:** This cable connects your MacBook to the power adapter, kind of like the cord that connects a lamp to an outlet.

Take everything out and place it on a clean, flat surface. Take a moment to admire how elegant and thoughtfully designed everything is. Apple's packaging is simple and clutter-free—everything has a place, and there's no extra fluff. This simplicity is part of Apple's philosophy: to make technology easy to understand and use right from the start.

Charging Your MacBook

Before we dive into the fun stuff, let's make sure your MacBook has enough power. Think of this step like filling up your car's gas tank before a road trip—you want to be fully fueled for the journey ahead!

Here's how to charge your MacBook:

1. Connect one end of the charging cable to the power adapter (the larger block).

2. Plug the other end of the cable into your MacBook's charging port.

3. Finally, connect the power adapter to a wall outlet.

If your MacBook uses a **MagSafe charger**, look for the small light on the connector. An amber light means your MacBook is charging, and a green light means it's fully charged. However, if your MacBook uses a **USB-C charger**, you won't see a light indicator. Instead, you can check the battery icon on your screen once the MacBook is powered on.

As you wait for your MacBook to charge, take a moment to get acquainted with its buttons and ports. Depending on your model, you'll see a few key features:

- **USB-C ports:** These are your MacBook's multitaskers. They handle charging, connecting to external monitors, and plugging in accessories—think of them as the Swiss Army knife of ports.

- **A headphone jack:** Perfect for plugging in headphones to enjoy your favorite music, podcasts, or FaceTime calls.

- **MagSafe charging port (on some models):** This specialized port securely connects your charger to your MacBook, snapping into place like magic.

Finding the Power Button and Turning It On

Now it's time to wake up your MacBook! Think of this step like turning the key in a car's ignition—this is where the adventure officially begins.

The power button is in the top-right corner of your MacBook's keyboard. On some models, it's a round button; on others, it's a black square that doubles as the Touch ID sensor. On newer MacBooks with a Touch Bar, the power button is part of the Touch ID button.

Some MacBooks even turn on automatically when you open the lid or connect them to a power source. If your MacBook doesn't power on right away, press the power button once and wait a few seconds. The screen will come to life with the iconic Apple logo and a cheerful BRIIIING sound, like an engine revving up.

If nothing happens, it might mean the battery needs more charge. Double-check that the charging cable is securely connected, then try again. Remember, even tech pros have moments where they wonder, "Is it plugged in?"

Initial Setup Steps: Language and Region

Once your MacBook powers on, it'll want to get to know you better. Think of this step as introducing yourself—it's how your MacBook learns where you are and how you want to communicate.

The first screen you'll see asks you to select a language. Here's how to navigate this step:

1. Use the **trackpad** (the rectangular touchpad below the keyboard) to move the cursor, the little arrow on the screen. Simply slide your finger across the trackpad, and the cursor will follow.

2. Click on your preferred language by pressing down gently on the trackpad—it works like a mouse.

Next, you'll be prompted to choose your region. This step ensures your MacBook knows your time zone, preferred date format, and whether to use Celsius or Fahrenheit. Once you've selected your region, click **Continue.**

Don't worry if you need to make changes later. You can adjust these settings anytime by going to the Apple menu, selecting **System Settings** (or **System Preferences** on older macOS versions), and choosing **Language & Region** in the sidebar.

That's it—you've completed the first step of setting up your MacBook!

Celebrate Your Progress

Take a deep breath and give yourself a pat on the back—you've unboxed, charged, and powered on your MacBook, and you've already started the setup process. This is a big deal! Learning something new can feel intimidating, but you're making great progress.

Think of this as the first step in becoming a MacBook Pro (another computer pun—you'll get used to those). Each small step forward builds your confidence, and I'll be right here with you to guide you through the next one.

Let's Keep Going

Your MacBook is ready for its next steps, and so are you. Together, we'll dive deeper into getting your device set up and personalized just the way you like it.

You're doing an amazing job so far, and I'm so proud of how far you've already come.

Let's keep the momentum going—you've got this!

GETTING ONLINE

CONNECTING YOUR MACBOOK TO THE WORLD

Think of Wi-Fi as an invisible magic bridge that connects your MacBook to the rest of the world. Without it, you couldn't browse the web, send emails, or video chat with your loved ones. In other words, it's essential—and setting it up is easier than you might think. Let's get your MacBook online and ready to explore all it can do.

How to Connect to Wi-Fi

1. Find the Wi-Fi Icon

In the top-right corner of your screen, you'll see an icon that looks like a fan or radar wave—this is your Wi-Fi indicator. Clicking on it will bring up a list of nearby networks. Think of it like tuning into a radio station, but instead of music, you're connecting to the internet.

2. Choose Your Network

Look through the list of networks for your home's Wi-Fi. It might be named after your internet provider or something more personal, like "Smith Family Wi-Fi." Click on the one that belongs to you.

3. Enter Your Wi-Fi Password

Once you click your network, a box will pop up asking for the Wi-Fi password. This step is like opening a locked gate—you'll need the key to get in. If you're not sure what the password is, check the sticker on the bottom of your Wi-Fi router or the paperwork from your internet provider. Wi-Fi passwords often include a mix of letters and numbers, so take your time and enter it carefully.

4. Click "Join"

After entering the password, click **Join.** If everything goes well, the Wi-Fi icon will fill in with black bars, showing you're connected. Hooray! You're officially online and ready to explore.

5. What If I Make a Mistake?

If you accidentally type the wrong password, don't worry—it happens to everyone! Simply try again. Letters like "O" and "0" or "l" and "1" can be tricky to tell apart, so double-check if you're having trouble. The good news? Once your MacBook connects, it will remember the network and password, so you won't need to enter it again.

Troubleshooting Common Wi-Fi Issues

Even after following all the steps, you might run into some hiccups. Don't worry—this happens to everyone, and it's usually easy to fix. Here are a few common problems and how to solve them:

Can't Find Your Network?

If your Wi-Fi network isn't visible, try moving closer to your router. Walls or other electronics can sometimes weaken the signal, just like trying to hear someone calling from another room. Getting closer makes it easier to connect.

Wrong Password?

If your MacBook says the password is incorrect, double-check the one you entered. Look for letters and numbers that might be easy to confuse, like "O" and "0" or "B" and "8." Take your time and try again.

Still Not Connecting?

Sometimes, all it takes is turning the Wi-Fi off and back on again. Click the Wi-Fi icon, select **Turn Wi-Fi Off**, wait a few seconds, and then click **Turn Wi-Fi On.** Think of it as giving your MacBook a little reset—it's surprising how often this works!

Restart Your Router

Your Wi-Fi router might need a quick break, too. Unplug it, wait about 10 seconds, then plug it back in. It may take a few minutes to restart, but this trick often solves stubborn connection issues.

Temporary Internet Outage?

If you've tried everything and your MacBook still won't connect, it could be an issue with your internet provider. These things happen! Give it a little time, and if the problem persists, you can call customer service for help. Remember, it's okay to ask for help—everyone needs it sometimes, especially with technology.

Celebrate Your Progress

You did it—you're officially online! This is a big step toward mastering your MacBook, and I couldn't be prouder of you. High five from your digital grandson!

Getting connected means the world is now at your fingertips. From FaceTiming your grandkids to discovering new recipes, you're ready to explore, learn, and stay in touch with the people who matter most.

In the next chapter, we'll set up your Apple ID, which unlocks all the incredible features your MacBook has to offer. But for now, give yourself a well-earned pat on the back. You're doing amazing, and I'm so excited to keep going on this journey with you!

What Is an Apple ID, and Why Do I Need One?

Unlocking the Magic of Your MacBook

Before we dive into creating your Apple ID, let's talk about what it is and why it's so important. Think of your Apple ID as the key to your MacBook's treasure chest. It unlocks all the amazing features your MacBook offers, like downloading apps, making FaceTime video calls, and storing photos and files in iCloud. Without it, your MacBook is like a TV without a remote—you can technically use it, but you'll miss out on all the fun.

Your Apple ID is your personal account that connects all your Apple devices and services. If you have an iPhone or an iPad, your Apple ID brings them together. Photos, contacts, reminders, and more will stay in sync across all your devices—like having a reliable old Rolodex that updates itself automatically, no matter where you add new information. Syncing simply means that the same information is available across all your devices. For example, syncing your contacts ensures that your address book stays identical on your MacBook, iPhone, and iPad, so you never lose touch with anyone important.

Your Apple ID also personalizes your MacBook experience. It remembers your preferences and keeps everything secure, like walking into your favorite diner where the staff already knows your order. It's one of the reasons Apple devices feel so intuitive and tailored just for you.

If you already have an Apple ID, go ahead and sign in. If not, let's create one together—I promise I'll make it as simple as possible!

Step-by-Step: Creating Your Apple ID

Let's create your Apple ID! Think of this process as filling out a quick form at the doctor's office—just a few questions to get you set up.

1. Open the Apple ID setup screen. If you didn't sign in during the initial setup, you can easily find it. Type Command + Spacebar to open Spotlight Search, a powerful tool on your MacBook that helps you find anything in an instant. Type "Apple ID" and press Return.

2. Click "Create a New Apple ID." This will bring up a screen asking for basic information, such as your name, birthday, and email address.

3. Enter your email address. Your email address will serve as your Apple ID. If you already have an email address, enter it here. If you don't, follow the on-screen directions to create a free iCloud email.

4. Create a strong password. Your password is like the lock on your front door—it protects all your information. A strong password includes letters, numbers, and maybe even a symbol or two. Choose something memorable but difficult for others to guess. If you're worried about forgetting it, jot it down in a secure spot—perhaps alongside those extra keys in the "just in case" drawer.

5. Agree to the Terms and Conditions. You'll be asked to agree to Apple's Terms and Conditions. These agreements may seem long, but they exist to protect your privacy and security. If you don't want to read the whole thing, just know that Apple takes these matters seriously. When you're ready, click Agree to continue.

Setting Up Security Questions

Apple will now prompt you to set up security questions. Think of these as extra locks for your front door in case you forget your password. Choose questions that only you would know the answers to, like:

- What was the name of your first pet?

- What street did you grow up on?

These questions ensure that even if someone tries to pretend they're you, they won't get far. Take your time choosing answers you'll remember years from now, and consider writing them down in a secure location, just in case.

If you ever need to update your security settings, you can do so in System Settings. Apple gives you the flexibility to adjust these questions as needed, which means one less thing to worry about.

What Happens Next?

With your Apple ID created, you've unlocked the door to all the amazing features of your MacBook. Now you can download apps from the App Store, make FaceTime video calls, and store photos and files in iCloud. iCloud is Apple's cloud storage service that acts like a secure, digital safe deposit box. It keeps your files, photos, and even contacts safe while making them accessible across all your Apple devices.

One of the best parts about having an Apple ID is how it syncs all your devices. Imagine taking a photo on your iPhone and seeing it instantly appear on your MacBook. It's like having a personal assistant who keeps everything organized for you.

Celebrate Your Progress

Take a moment to celebrate—you've just created your Apple ID, and that's no small feat! This may seem like a small step, but it's actually a big leap toward mastering your MacBook.

With each step you take, you're building confidence and gaining skills that will make your MacBook experience more rewarding. Remember, there's no rush. If you ever need to revisit these steps or ask for help, that's okay—learning is a journey, and I'm here with you every step of the way.

Now that your Apple ID is ready, we're one step closer to unlocking the full potential of your MacBook. Let's keep going—you're doing amazing!

MAKING YOUR MACBOOK MORE ACCESSIBLE

VISION, HEARING, AND INTERACTION FEATURES

Your MacBook is designed to be user-friendly for everyone, offering features that make it easier to see, hear, and use. Accessibility settings let you customize your MacBook to suit your unique needs, making it more comfortable and personalized. Think of these features as adjustments to a new car—tweaking the mirrors, seat, and radio stations until everything feels just right.

Let's explore how to access these powerful tools and make your MacBook feel like it was built just for you.

Finding Accessibility Settings

To start, we'll locate the Accessibility menu. You can do this in a couple of ways, but here's the easiest:

- Open **Spotlight Search** by pressing Command + Spacebar. This handy tool is like a magnifying glass that helps you find anything on your MacBook.

- Type "Accessibility" and press Return.

You'll see the Accessibility settings window pop up, neatly organized into categories: vision, hearing, and motor. Feel free to click around—it's like exploring drawers in a new kitchen. You'll soon get a sense of where everything is, and I'll guide you through the most useful features step by step.

Adjusting Text Size and Display

Have you ever found yourself squinting at your screen or leaning in a little too close? Let's make everything easier on your eyes by adjusting how text and visuals appear.

1. **Select Display**: In the Accessibility settings, find and click "Display" in the left-hand column.

2. **Adjust the Text Size**: Use the text size slider to make the text bigger or smaller. Slide it to the right to increase the size or to the left to reduce it. It's like adjusting the headline on a newspaper—make it as big as you need!

3. **Increase Contrast**: If items on the screen blend together, enabling "Increase Contrast" can make them pop. It's like darkening the print to improve readability.

4. **Invert Colors**: For those who find bright screens uncomfortable, the "Invert Colors" option softens the display. It's like switching to night-time mode—gentler on your eyes and perfect for extended use.

If you want to go a step further, consider adjusting the cursor size. A larger cursor can be easier to track on a busy screen. You'll find the cursor size slider in the Display section. Make it as big as you like—it's like finding your favorite pen on a cluttered desk.

Additional Accessibility Tools

Your MacBook has even more features to make it comfortable to use. Let's look at a few favorites:

- **Zoom**: Need to take a closer look? Enable Zoom in the Accessibility settings. Then, press Command and Option together and hit the + key to zoom in or the - key to zoom out. It's like using a magnifying glass to see the fine print.

- **Hover Text**: With Hover Text enabled, hover your mouse over any text to see a larger version appear. It's like having magic reading glasses that follow your cursor. To enable it, go to the Zoom section and check the box labeled "Enable Hover Text."

- **Dictation**: If you'd rather speak than type, Dictation has you covered. Go to System Settings > Keyboard > Dictation and turn it on. Once enabled, press the Fn key twice to start dictating. It's like having a personal assistant jot down your thoughts.

- **Reduce Motion**: Some animations, like windows zooming in and out, can feel distracting or dizzying. Enable "Reduce Motion" in the Display section to simplify screen movements, making them calmer and easier to follow.

- **VoiceOver**: If you have trouble seeing the screen, VoiceOver is a built-in screen reader that describes what's happening. Navigate to Accessibility > VoiceOver to enable it. A built-in tutorial will walk you through how to use it—it's like having a coach guide you step by step.

- **Sticky Keys**: If pressing multiple keys at once is challenging, Sticky Keys can help. For example, instead of pressing Command + Shift + 4 all at once to take a screenshot, you can press each key individually, and your MacBook will remember them. Enable this feature in Accessibility > Keyboard > Sticky Keys.

- **Slow Keys**: For those who press keys too quickly by accident, Slow Keys adds a slight delay before recognizing a key press. It's like giving yourself a moment to think before acting, which can help reduce errors.

Celebrate Your Progress

Congratulations! You've just explored some of the most powerful accessibility tools your MacBook offers. Whether you've adjusted the text size, enabled Dictation, or tried out Zoom, you're taking steps to make your MacBook work for *you*.

These features aren't just about making your MacBook easier to use—they're about enhancing your comfort, confidence, and independence. It's like customizing your favorite chair or finding the perfect lighting in a room—small adjustments make a world of difference.

Take a moment to appreciate how far you've come. You're not just learning how to use your MacBook; you're transforming it into a tool that fits your needs perfectly. Let's keep going—there's so much more to discover!

Navigating the MacBook Interface

DIGITAL GRANDSON PRESS

UNDERSTANDING YOUR MACBOOK DESKTOP, DOCK, AND MENU BAR

ORGANIZE YOUR DIGITAL WORKSPACE

Welcome to the heart of your MacBook—the desktop! Think of it as your personal digital workspace, where you can organize files, launch apps, and customize everything to suit your preferences. Just like arranging your physical desk, a little organization here goes a long way in making your MacBook easy to use and uniquely yours.

Let's explore how to make the desktop, Dock, and Menu Bar work for you, step by step.

The Desktop: Your Digital Workspace

When you first start your MacBook, the desktop appears as a clean slate. You'll see a background image, usually a scenic landscape or pattern, but don't worry—you can change it later to a favorite family photo or something that makes you smile.

Your desktop acts like the top of a physical desk: a space where you can store files, folders, and shortcuts to important documents for quick access. But, like a real desk, too much clutter can make things harder to find.

Here are some key ways to make your desktop neat and useful:

- **Drag and Drop Files:** You can move files or folders onto the desktop by clicking and holding, dragging them to a new location, and then letting go. It's like picking up a book from one shelf and placing it on another.

- **Create Shortcuts with Aliases:** If you want quick access to a file without keeping it on the desktop, create an alias. Right-click the file, select "Make Alias," and drag the alias to your desktop. This keeps the original file in its folder while giving you a handy shortcut.

Tips for Staying Organized on the Desktop:

- Use **folders** to group related files, like work documents, photos, or recipes. Right-click on the desktop and select "New Folder."

- Enable **Stacks** to keep similar files (like screenshots or PDFs) grouped together. Right-click the desktop and choose "Use Stacks."

- Limit clutter by keeping only current files on the desktop, like your active projects. Move completed items to folders, much like tidying up a kitchen counter at the end of the day.

- Change your background by right-clicking the desktop and selecting "Change Desktop Background." A personal image can make your MacBook feel even more like home.

The Dock: Your Quick Access Tool

The Dock, located at the bottom of your screen, is like your MacBook's toolbox. It gives you quick access to your favorite apps and tools, just like keeping frequently used items—like coffee or your phone charger—on your kitchen counter. Let's customize it so it works best for you.

- **Add Apps to the Dock:** Open an app, right-click (or Control + Click) on its icon in the Dock, and select "Options" > "Keep in Dock." Now the app will stay in the Dock even after you close it.

- **Remove Apps from the Dock:** Click and drag an app's icon out of the Dock until you see a small "Remove" label. Let go, and the app disappears from the Dock—but don't worry, it's still in the Applications folder.

- **Rearrange the Dock:** Click and drag icons to rearrange them in any order. Put your most-used apps front and center, like organizing your spice rack so the essentials are always within reach.

- **Resize the Dock:** To make the icons larger or smaller, go to **Apple Menu (□)** > **System Settings** > **Desktop & Dock**, and adjust the size slider.

- **Enable Automatic Hiding:** To free up screen space, set the Dock to hide when not in use. Go to **System Settings** > **Desktop & Dock** and enable "Automatically hide and show the Dock." The Dock will slide out of view until you move your cursor to the bottom of the screen.

The Menu Bar: Your Control Panel

The Menu Bar runs along the top of your screen and is packed with shortcuts to essential tools and settings. Think of it as the control panel of your MacBook, giving you easy access to what you need.

- **Apple Menu:** Located in the far-left corner, the Apple icon opens key options like **About This Mac**, **System Settings**, and **Shut Down.** It's like the front door of your house—your starting point for important tasks.

- **App Menus:** Next to the Apple menu, you'll see menus specific to the app you're using, such as File, Edit, and View in Safari. These provide quick access to app-specific functions, like saving documents or printing pages.

- **Status Icons:** On the right side of the Menu Bar, you'll find icons for Wi-Fi, Bluetooth, battery status, and the clock. Clicking these lets you check and adjust settings quickly. For example, click the Wi-Fi icon to connect to a network or check your signal strength.

- **Spotlight Search:** The magnifying glass icon opens Spotlight Search, a powerful tool to find files, apps, or even web content. If you ever lose track of something, Spotlight will help you find it in seconds.

- **Control Center:** The Control Center icon, resembling two sliders, gives you quick access to features like volume, brightness, and Wi-Fi. It's like having a mini dashboard to adjust settings on the fly.

Celebrate Your Progress

Congratulations! You've mastered the basics of your desktop, Dock, and Menu Bar—three essential parts of your MacBook. Each adjustment you've made brings you closer to a MacBook that's perfectly tailored to your needs.

By organizing your desktop, customizing the Dock, and getting familiar with the Menu Bar, you've set the stage for smoother, more enjoyable use. Remember, there's no rush. Take your time to explore, tweak, and make your MacBook truly yours.

You're doing an amazing job, and with every step, you're becoming more confident and capable. Let's keep going—there's so much more to discover!

HOW TO USE FINDER TO MANAGE YOUR FILES

If the desktop is your MacBook's workspace, Finder is the magical filing cabinet that keeps everything behind the scenes organized. Think of Finder as your MacBook's librarian—it helps you locate, sort, and manage all your files and folders. Whether it's photos, documents, or apps, Finder is your go-to tool for keeping everything tidy and easy to find.

Let's explore how Finder works and how to make the most of its powerful features.

Opening Finder

Finder is always just a click away. To open it, look for the blue and white **Finder icon** in your Dock—it looks like a friendly smiling face. When you click it, a Finder window will open, displaying all your files and folders. It's like opening a filing cabinet drawer: everything is ready for you to browse.

Once you get the hang of Finder, finding files will feel as intuitive as flipping through a well-organized Rolodex—just faster and less prone to paper cuts!

Creating and Organizing Folders

One of the best ways to keep your digital life in order is by creating folders for related files. Think of this like using labeled drawers in a filing cabinet. Without them, everything would pile up in one chaotic mess, making it impossible to find what you need.

- **Creating a Folder**: Open Finder and navigate to the location where you want the folder. Right-click (or Control + Click) and select "New Folder." A blank folder will appear, ready to be named. Use descriptive names like "Vacation Photos" or "Tax Documents" so you'll know exactly what's inside without opening it.

- **Moving Files into Folders**: Drag and drop files into your new folder by clicking and holding a file, dragging it to the folder, and letting go. It's as simple as moving papers from your desk into a labeled folder.

- **Creating Subfolders**: If a folder starts filling up, create subfolders to keep things even more organized. For example, in your "Work Documents" folder, you might create subfolders for "Reports" and "Meeting Notes." Think of it like adding dividers to a filing cabinet drawer—it makes finding things even easier.

- **Renaming Folders**: To rename a folder, click on it once, wait a moment, then click again to start typing a new name. Clear labels save time later when you're hunting for files.

Pro Tip: Keep your folders organized by sorting their contents. In Finder, go to the **View** menu and select **Sort By** to arrange files by name, date, type, or size. It's like sorting a stack of papers on your desk into neat categories.

Searching for Files

Even with an organized system, it's easy to misplace a file. That's where Finder's search bar comes to the rescue.

- **Using the Search Bar**: Open a Finder window and type a keyword into the search bar in the top-right corner. Finder will instantly display files that match your search term. You can search by filename or even by text inside a document. It's like having a metal detector at the beach—if it's there, Finder will help you uncover it.

- **Narrowing Your Search**: Too many results? Use filters to narrow things down. Finder lets you filter by file type (like documents or images) or by the date the file was last opened. It's like flipping to the right section of a phone book instead of reading every name.

- **Advanced Search Criteria**: For an even more precise search, click the plus (+) button next to the search bar to add criteria like file size, creation date, or tags. It's like giving Finder a detailed set of instructions to find exactly what you need.

- **Saving Searches**: If you frequently search for the same types of files, save time by saving the search. After filtering your results, click the **Save** button to create a shortcut in the Finder sidebar. It's like leaving a bookmark in your favorite book so you can return to it quickly.

Using Tags and Shortcuts

Tags and shortcuts make managing files even easier, helping you find what you need at a glance.

- **Tagging Files**: Tags act like color-coded sticky notes for your files. Right-click a file, select a tag color, and later click that color in the Finder sidebar to see all tagged files in one place. For example, you might use red for important documents or green for vacation plans. It's a simple way to group files without moving them into folders.

- **Creating Shortcuts (Aliases)**: If you frequently access a file or folder, create an alias—a shortcut that stays in an easily accessible spot, like your desktop. Right-click the file, select "Make Alias," and move the alias wherever you want. The original file stays safely in its folder, but the alias gives you quick access.

Pro Tip: Add your most-used folders to the Finder sidebar for instant access. Drag a folder into the sidebar, and it'll always be just a click away.

Smart Folders and Quick Look

Finder has a few extra tricks up its sleeve to help you stay organized and save time.

- **Smart Folders**: A Smart Folder automatically collects files based on criteria you set, like file type or creation date. For example, you could create a Smart Folder that shows all your PDF files, no matter where they're stored. To make one, go to **File > New Smart Folder**, set your criteria, and click Save. It's like hiring a digital assistant to organize your files for you.

- **Quick Look**: Need to check if a file is the right one? Select it in Finder and press the spacebar to preview it without opening the app. Quick Look works with documents, images, and even videos. It's like flipping through a book before deciding to read it.

Celebrate Your Progress

You've just unlocked the power of Finder, your MacBook's ultimate organizational tool! By learning how to create folders, use tags, and customize your searches, you're turning your MacBook into a well-oiled machine.

Each time you organize files or find something quickly with Finder, you're saving time and building confidence. And remember, an organized MacBook isn't just efficient—it's stress-free and satisfying to use.

You're doing an amazing job, and your digital filing cabinet is shaping up beautifully. Let's keep going—there's so much more to explore!

Mastering System Settings

Adjusting Display, Sound, and Text for Comfort and Ease

System Settings are like your MacBook's command center. It's where you can fine-tune everything to suit your needs—adjusting brightness, sound, text size, and more. Think of it as setting up a new car: you want the seat, mirrors, and radio adjusted just right to make the ride smooth and enjoyable. With System Settings, you can make your MacBook work exactly how you want it to.

Let's dive in and explore how to access and personalize your MacBook's settings step by step.

Opening System Settings

There are two easy ways to open System Settings:

1. **From the Apple Menu:** Click the Apple icon in the upper-left corner of your screen, then select **System Settings**.

2. **From the Dock:** Look for the icon that resembles a set of gears. Clicking it will take you straight to System Settings.

Once inside, you'll see a sidebar filled with categories for different settings. It might look like a lot at first, but don't worry—it's like learning a new remote control. Once you get the hang of it, navigating System Settings will feel second nature.

If you're not sure where to find a setting, use the **search bar** at the top of the window. Type what you're looking for, like "brightness" or "volume," and it will take you directly to the right place. Think of it as your settings GPS—no more getting lost in the menus.

Adjusting Display Settings and Brightness

Your MacBook's display settings let you see everything clearly and comfortably. Whether you're working in a bright room or winding down at night, tweaking the display can make all the difference.

- **Adjusting Brightness:** Go to **System Settings > Displays.** Use the brightness slider to make your screen brighter or dimmer. Move it to the right to brighten the display and to the left to dim it. It's like adjusting the lights in your living room—find the setting that's most comfortable for your eyes.

- **Night Shift:** For evening use, enable **Night Shift** to warm up the colors on your screen, reducing blue light that can strain your eyes. In **Displays**, click **Night Shift** and set it to turn on automatically at sunset or during specific hours. It's like switching to softer lighting after dark—easy on the eyes and helps you relax.

- **True Tone:** If your MacBook supports it, turn on **True Tone** to adjust your screen's color temperature based on the room's lighting. This makes the display look more natural and reduces eye strain. You'll find this option under **System Settings > Displays.**

Changing Sound Preferences and Volume

Your MacBook's sound settings control everything from music playback to notification alerts. Let's make sure everything sounds just right for you.

- **Adjusting Volume:** Go to **System Settings** > **Sound** and use the volume slider to set the sound level. You can also use the volume keys on your keyboard (usually on the top row) for quick adjustments.

- **Choosing an Output Device:** If you're using headphones or external speakers, select them as your output device under the **Output** tab in the Sound menu. It's like connecting headphones to a stereo—just tell your MacBook where to send the sound!

- **Alert Sounds:** Customize the sounds your MacBook makes for notifications. Under the **Sound Effects** tab, choose a tone that you like or turn alerts off for a quieter workspace. It's like picking a ringtone for your phone—find something pleasant, or enjoy the peace of silence.

- **Input Device (Microphone):** If you need to use a microphone for video calls, select the **Input** tab in the Sound menu. You can adjust the input level to ensure your voice comes through clearly, like making sure you're not whispering across a noisy room.

Personalizing Fonts and Text Size

Making the text on your MacBook easier to read can transform your experience, especially if smaller fonts strain your eyes.

- **Adjusting System Text Size:** While macOS doesn't have a universal text size slider, you can enlarge text in some areas. Go to **System Settings** > **Accessibility** > **Display** and enable **Larger Text.** This increases the size of menu text and certain interface elements, making everything more comfortable to read.

- **Finder and Mail Text Size:** Apps like Finder and Mail let you adjust text sizes individually. In Finder, go to **View > Show View Options** to change the text size for files and folders. In Mail, open **Mail > Preferences > Fonts & Colors** to choose larger fonts for emails.

- **Zoom:** If you need to magnify part of the screen, enable the Zoom feature under **System Settings > Accessibility > Zoom.** Use the keyboard shortcuts **Option + Command +** = to zoom in and **Option + Command + -** to zoom out. It's like using a magnifying glass for a closer look.

- **Safari Reader Mode:** When reading online, Safari's Reader Mode simplifies web pages by enlarging text and removing distractions. Click the Reader icon (a page symbol with lines) in the address bar to enable it. It's like clearing a cluttered desk so you can focus on the task at hand.

- **App-Specific Fonts:** Some apps, like Notes, let you customize fonts directly. Open Notes, click **Format > Font**, and select a style and size that's easiest for you to read.

Celebrate Your Progress

You've done an amazing job exploring System Settings! From adjusting display brightness to customizing text size and sound preferences, you've taken important steps to make your MacBook more comfortable and tailored to your needs.

Each tweak you make brings you closer to a MacBook experience that feels truly yours. Remember, there's no rush—take your time to explore these settings and revisit them as you get more comfortable.

You're doing fantastic, and I'm so proud of the progress you're making. Let's keep moving forward—there's so much more to discover together!

Getting Started with Siri

Your Personal Assistant for Daily Tasks

Siri is like having a helpful assistant built right into your MacBook. Whether you need to set reminders, search the web, send messages, or just hear a good joke, Siri is there to make your life easier. Think of Siri as the grandchild who always knows the answers and never gets tired of helping out—no eye rolls included!

In this chapter, we'll set up Siri, explore what she can do, and customize her features to fit your needs.

Setting Up Siri on Your MacBook

Before Siri can start lending a hand, you'll need to set her up. Thankfully, it's much easier than the gadgets of the past—no wires or complicated manuals here!

1. **Enable Siri**:

   - Click the **Apple menu** in the top-left corner of your screen and select **System Settings.**

   - In the sidebar, scroll down and click **Siri.**

   - Toggle the switch next to **Siri** to turn it on.

2. **Choose Your Activation Method**:

   ○ If your MacBook supports it, toggle on **Listen for "Hey Siri."** Once enabled, you can simply say, "Hey Siri," and she'll be ready to help. When Siri is listening, you'll see a glowing orb or waveform at the bottom center of your screen.

   ○ Prefer not to use voice activation? Set a **Keyboard Shortcut** instead. You can customize this shortcut in the same settings menu. For example, you might choose to press and hold the **Command + Spacebar** keys to activate Siri.

Pro Tip: Siri requires an internet connection to work. Make sure you're connected to Wi-Fi for the best experience.

Using Siri for Daily Tasks

Siri is a jack-of-all-trades when it comes to simplifying your day. From setting reminders to sending messages, she's ready to assist. Here are a few examples:

- **Set Reminders and Alarms**:

   ○ Need to remember to take your medication at 3 PM? Just say, "Hey Siri, remind me to take my medicine at 3 PM." Siri will set a reminder that pops up right on schedule. Think of it as tying a string around your finger—but without the string.

- **Search the Web**:

   ○ Want to know the weather forecast or when Casablanca was released? Just ask, "Hey Siri, what's the weather like today?" or "Hey Siri, when did Casablanca come out?" Siri will find the answer for you, often without needing a full web search. It's like having an encyclopedia that talks back.

- **Send Messages Hands-Free**:

  ○ If your hands are busy, Siri can send messages for you. Say, "Hey Siri, send a message to Sarah," and then dictate your message. Siri will confirm the details before sending it, ensuring there are no mistakes. It's like having a secretary on call to handle your typing.

Voice Command Tips

Getting used to Siri is easy, but a few tips can make the process smoother:

- **Speak Naturally**: No need to use robotic phrases or special commands. Talk to Siri like you would a friend: "Hey Siri, what time is it?" or "Hey Siri, send an email to John about dinner plans." She's surprisingly good at understanding natural speech.

- **Keep Commands Simple at First**: If you're just starting out, stick with straightforward commands like setting a timer or checking the weather. As you get more comfortable, you can experiment with more complex tasks.

- **Rephrase When Needed**: If Siri doesn't understand you the first time, that's okay! Simply rephrase or speak more clearly. Think of it like talking to someone in a noisy café—sometimes you just have to repeat yourself.

Discovering Siri's Hidden Talents

Siri is more than just practical—she's fun, too! Try asking Siri to tell you a joke, play your favorite music, or even solve a quick math problem.

Here are a few ideas to explore:

- "Hey Siri, play some jazz."

- "Hey Siri, what's 547 divided by 13?"

- "Hey Siri, tell me a joke."

The more you use Siri, the more you'll discover what she can do. She's always learning and improving, making her a helpful companion as you navigate your MacBook.

Celebrate Your Progress

Congratulations! You've just unlocked one of your MacBook's most convenient features. Siri is here to help with everything from reminders to jokes, and each new task you master brings you closer to making the most of your MacBook.

Take a moment to celebrate how far you've come—you're learning more every day, and Siri is just one of the many tools in your growing MacBook toolkit. Keep practicing, exploring, and asking questions. The more you use Siri, the more confident you'll feel.

Great work, and let's keep this journey going—you're doing amazing!

Organizing and Managing Photos

DIGITAL GRANDSON PRESS

IMPORTING AND ORGANIZING YOUR PHOTOS

SAVE, SORT, AND RELIVE YOUR FAVORITE MEMORIES

Capturing special moments is one thing—getting them onto your MacBook and organizing them is another! Whether you're transferring photos from your iPhone or a camera, your MacBook makes it easy to store and sort them, so they're always right where you need them.

In this chapter, we'll go over how to connect your device, import photos using the Photos app, and organize them into albums so you can easily find your favorite moments. Let's get started!

Connecting Your iPhone or Camera to Your MacBook

Before you can transfer photos, you need to connect your device to your Mac-Book. Think of it like plugging in a toaster before making toast—nothing happens without that connection!

Step 1: Connect Your iPhone or Camera

- **For an iPhone**: Use the **Lightning-to-USB** cable (the same one you use to charge your phone). Plug one end into your iPhone and the other into your MacBook's USB or USB-C port (you may need an adapter if your MacBook only has USB-C).

- **For a Camera**: Use the **USB cable** that came with your camera. If your camera uses an SD card, you can also insert the card directly into your MacBook's SD card slot (if available) or use an external SD card reader.

Step 2: Trust This Computer (For iPhones Only)

- When you connect your iPhone for the first time, a message will pop up on your iPhone asking, **"Trust This Computer?"**

- Tap **"Trust"** and enter your passcode. This lets your MacBook access your photos—think of it like introducing two friends so they can start sharing with each other!

Step 3: Turn On Your Camera (For Cameras Only)

- If you're using a camera, make sure it's turned on. Some cameras also require you to select a **transfer mode**—check your camera's screen for any prompts and select the appropriate option (often labeled **"PC Mode"** or **"Transfer"**).

Once connected, your MacBook will recognize the device, and you'll be ready to start importing your photos!

Using the Photos App to Import Photos

Now that your device is connected, let's transfer your pictures into the **Photos app**, where they'll be safely stored and easy to find. Think of this step as taking photos out of a shoebox and neatly placing them into albums.

Step 1: Open the Photos App

- Click the **Photos** icon in your Dock, or open **Spotlight Search** (Command + Spacebar) and type **"Photos."**

Step 2: Select Your Device

- If the import screen doesn't appear automatically, look at the **left sidebar** in the Photos app and click on your device under **Devices.**

Step 3: Choose Photos to Import

- Your Photos app will display all the images available for import. You can:

  - Click **"Import All New Photos"** to transfer everything that hasn't already been saved.

  - Select individual photos by clicking on them, then click **"Import Selected."**

Step 4: Wait for the Transfer to Complete

- A small progress indicator will show you how long the import will take. Once done, your photos will be saved in the **Library** section of the Photos app.

Your pictures are now safely stored on your MacBook—like transferring them from a camera to a beautifully arranged photo album!

Organizing Photos into Albums

Now that your photos are on your MacBook, let's organize them so you can easily find your favorite moments later. Albums help group photos by event, person, or theme—like different sections in a scrapbook.

Step 1: Create a New Album

- Open the **Photos app**, click **File** in the top menu, then select **"New Album."**

- A blank album will appear—give it a descriptive name, like **"Family Reunion 2024"** or **"Hawaii Vacation."**

Step 2: Add Photos to an Album

- Click on the **Library** section in the sidebar.

- Find the images you want to group together, then:

  - **Drag them** into the album you just created, OR

  - **Right-click the photos**, choose **"Add to,"** and select your album.

Step 3: Use Albums to Keep Track of Events

- Having separate albums for vacations, birthdays, or grandkid milestones makes it easy to relive specific memories. Instead of scrolling through thousands of photos, you can jump straight to the ones you want—like flipping right to the chapter of a book instead of reading the whole thing!

Sorting Photos by Date, People, and Keywords

The **Photos app** has built-in tools to help you quickly find images without manually sorting them.

View by Date

- Click **Library** > **Photos** to see your pictures automatically sorted in chronological order—like a timeline of your favorite moments.

Use the People Feature

- The **People** section in Photos recognizes faces and groups pictures of the same person together.

- Click **People** in the sidebar to see pre-sorted photo collections of your friends and family.

- You can **label** faces to make searching even easier! Just click on a person's album, type their name, and Photos will continue organizing new pictures of them in the future.

Search by Keyword

- You can assign **keywords** to photos to make them easier to find later.

- Click on a photo, then go to **Window** > **Info** (or press **Command + I**) to add a keyword, like **"Beach"** or **"Christmas 2023."**

- Later, just type that keyword in the search bar, and Photos will pull up every picture that matches.

Create Smart Albums for Automatic Organization

- A **Smart Album** automatically gathers photos that match certain rules—like all pictures from July 2024 or every photo tagged with "Birthday."

- To create one, click **File** > **New Smart Album**, then set conditions like **"Date is July 2024"** or **"Keyword contains Beach."**

- It's like having your own digital photo librarian keeping things organized for you!

Celebrate Your Progress

Congratulations! You've successfully imported, organized, and sorted your photos like a pro. Whether you're reminiscing about a special trip or looking up a grandkid's baby pictures, everything is now easy to find and enjoy.

Each step you've taken brings order to your digital photo collection, making it a joy to look back on your memories whenever you want.

Keep practicing, explore the Photos app, and enjoy reliving your favorite moments—your MacBook is now your personal photo album, beautifully arranged and ready whenever you are. Up next, we'll explore **editing tools** to make your pictures look even better! You've got this!

EDITING, ORGANIZING, AND SHARING YOUR PHOTOS

MAKE YOUR MEMORIES SHINE AND SHARE THEM WITH LOVED ONES

Your photos are more than just images—they're moments, memories, and little pieces of life you want to hold onto. The Photos app on your MacBook makes it easy to enhance, organize, and share your pictures so you can enjoy them for years to come.

In this chapter, we'll explore how to edit your photos to bring out their best, create albums to keep everything organized, and share your favorite snapshots with family and friends. Plus, we'll cover some common troubleshooting tips in case things don't go quite as planned. Let's get started!

Editing Your Photos with the Photos App

You don't need to be a professional photographer to make your pictures look great. The **Photos app** includes simple, powerful editing tools that let you brighten, crop, and enhance your images with just a few clicks.

Step 1: Open a Photo to Edit

- Open the **Photos app** and find the image you want to edit.

- Click on the photo, then click the **Edit** button in the **top-right corner** of the Photos window.

- Think of it like pulling a favorite picture out of a scrapbook to touch it up before putting it in a frame.

Step 2: Use Auto-Enhance for a Quick Fix

- Click the **Auto-Enhance** slider in the **Adjust** tab to let your MacBook automatically improve the brightness, contrast, and color of your photo.

- It's like giving your picture an instant refresh—like adjusting the blinds to let in just the right amount of light.

Step 3: Adjust Light and Color Manually

- Click **Adjust** to fine-tune brightness, contrast, highlights, and color.

- Use the sliders to tweak the image until it looks just right.

- Don't be afraid to experiment—you can always click **Revert to Original** if things don't go as planned.

Step 4: Crop and Rotate

- Use the **Crop** tool to remove distractions or straighten a tilted photo.

- Click **Rotate** to fix sideways images.

- It's like trimming a printed photo to fit perfectly into a frame—clean and polished.

Step 5: Apply Filters for a Unique Look

- Click **Filters** to try different styles, from bright and vivid to classic black and white.

- Want your sunset photo to pop? Try **Vivid Warm.** Prefer an old-time feel? **Mono** makes it black and white.

- Think of it like choosing the perfect frame to match the mood of your picture!

Editing should be fun—play around, try new things, and find the style that feels right for you.

Creating and Organizing Albums

Now that your photos look their best, let's organize them into **albums** so they're easy to find later. Albums help group related photos, like vacations, birthdays, or favorite everyday moments.

Step 1: Create a New Album

- Open the **Photos app** and click **File > New Album.**

- Give your album a name, like **"Grandkids' Visit 2024"** or **"Hawaii Vacation."**

- Think of this like labeling a folder in a photo album—you'll know exactly where to look when you want to revisit those memories.

Step 2: Add Photos to an Album

- Go to the **Library** section and find the photos you want to add.

- **Drag them** into your new album or **right-click** and select **"Add to"**, followed by the album name.

- **Important:** Your photos will **stay in the main Library**, even if they're in an album—think of albums as playlists rather than moving the originals.

Step 3: Use Smart Albums for Automatic Organization

- Want your MacBook to do the organizing for you? Create a **Smart Album**!

- Click **File** > **New Smart Album**, then set conditions like:

  - "Photos from July 2024"

  - "Photos with 'Beach' keyword"

  - "Favorites" (photos you've marked with a heart)

- The Photos app will automatically sort your pictures based on your rules—it's like having a personal assistant for your memories!

Sharing Your Photos with Family and Friends

One of the best parts of photography is sharing moments with loved ones. Whether you're sending a single snapshot or an entire album, your MacBook makes it easy.

Option 1: Share Individual Photos

- Select the photo(s) you want to share.

- Click the **Share** button (a small square with an arrow) in the **top-right corner.**

- Choose **Messages, Mail, or AirDrop** to send them quickly.

- It's like mailing a postcard—but instantly!

Option 2: Create a Shared Album in iCloud

- Want to share lots of photos at once? Use **iCloud Shared Albums.**

- Go to **Photos > Settings > iCloud**, then turn on **Shared Albums.**

- Click **Shared Albums** in the sidebar, then **Create a New Shared Album.**

- Enter email addresses for the people you want to invite.

- Now your friends and family can view, comment, and even add their own photos!

It's like having a digital scrapbook that updates itself—perfect for keeping in touch with grandkids or sharing vacation highlights.

Troubleshooting Common Photo Issues

Sometimes things don't go quite as planned. Here's how to fix common photo problems.

Problem: Photos Won't Import from iPhone

Solution:

- Make sure your iPhone is unlocked and shows **"Trust This Comput-**

er" when connected. Tap **Trust** and enter your passcode.

- Try using a different **USB cable or port** on your MacBook.

- If all else fails, restart both your **MacBook and iPhone** and try again.

Problem: Photos Aren't Showing in an Album

Solution:

- Double-check that you **dragged** the photos into the album or used **"Add to Album."**

- Restart the **Photos app** (press **Command + Q** to quit, then reopen).

- Remember: Photos **stay in the Library**, even if they're in albums.

Problem: iCloud Sharing Isn't Working

Solution:

- Go to **System Settings > Apple ID > iCloud > Photos** and make sure **Sync This Mac** is turned on.

- Check that **iCloud Shared Albums** is enabled under **Photos > Settings > iCloud.**

- If your internet is slow, large albums may take time to upload.

Problem: The Photos App Is Frozen

Solution:

- Try quitting the app by pressing **Command + Q.**

- If it won't quit, use **Force Quit (Option + Command + Escape)** and select **Photos.**

- Restart your MacBook if the problem persists—sometimes, it just needs a quick reset!

Celebrate Your Progress!

You've now mastered editing, organizing, and sharing your photos! Whether you're touching up a family picture, creating a special album, or sending memories to loved ones, you're making your MacBook work for you.

Take a moment to celebrate how far you've come—what once seemed overwhelming is now second nature. Keep experimenting, playing with filters, and finding new ways to enjoy your photos.

Next up, we'll dive into **iCloud backups**, so your memories are always safe and accessible. Keep up the fantastic work—you're doing great!

BACKING UP AND SYNCING PHOTOS WITH iCLOUD

KEEP YOUR MEMORIES SAFE AND ACCESSIBLE ANYTIME, ANYWHERE

Your photos are more than just digital files—they are memories, milestones, and moments you never want to lose. Whether it's a grandchild's first steps, a family reunion, or that stunning sunset from your last vacation, you want to keep them safe and easy to access.

That's where iCloud Photos comes in. With iCloud, your pictures are automatically backed up and synced across all your Apple devices. That means no more worrying about losing them if something happens to your MacBook—and no more emailing photos to yourself just to see them on your iPhone.

In this chapter, we'll go step by step through setting up iCloud, managing storage, and recovering deleted photos so you can feel confident that your precious memories are secure.

Setting Up iCloud Photos on Your MacBook

Before iCloud can do its job, you need to turn it on and make sure it is set up correctly.

Step 1: Open iCloud Settings

- Click the **Apple menu** in the top-left corner and select **System Settings** (**System Preferences** if you're using macOS Monterey or earlier).

- Click **Apple ID**, then **iCloud**.

Step 2: Turn On iCloud Photos

- Scroll down to **Photos** and toggle **Sync this Mac** to "On."

- This ensures that every photo you take on your iPhone or add to your MacBook is backed up and available on all your Apple devices.

Think of iCloud like a fireproof safe for your photos—it keeps them protected, no matter what happens to your MacBook.

Syncing Photos Across All Your Apple Devices

One of iCloud's best features is that it automatically syncs your photos across your iPhone, iPad, and MacBook. It's like having a magical photo album that follows you everywhere—no need to manually transfer anything.

Step 1: Check Your iPhone or iPad Settings

- On your **iPhone or iPad**, open **Settings** and tap your **name** at the top.

- Select **iCloud > Photos**, then make sure **Sync this iPhone/iPad** is turned on.

Step 2: Let iCloud Work Automatically

- Once iCloud Photos is enabled, every new picture you take will automatically appear on your MacBook—no cables, no extra steps.

- It's like having your favorite photos instantly framed and displayed in every room of your house without lifting a finger.

Step 3: Save Space with "Optimize Storage"

If you're worried about running out of space on your MacBook, iCloud offers an option called **Optimize Mac Storage**:

- This keeps full-resolution photos in iCloud while storing smaller, space-saving versions on your MacBook.

- Think of it like keeping original paintings in a museum while carrying a small photo album of them—you still have access to everything without taking up too much space.

To enable it:

- Go to **System Settings > Apple ID > iCloud > Photos**, then turn on **Optimize Mac Storage**.

Managing iCloud Storage Space

Now that your photos are safely backed up, let's make sure you have enough room for everything. iCloud gives you 5GB of free storage, but photos and videos can fill that up quickly.

Step 1: Check Your iCloud Storage

- Open **System Settings** > **Apple ID** > **iCloud** (or **System Preferences** > **iCloud** on older Macs).

- Click **Manage** to see how much space your photos are using.

Step 2: Upgrade Your Storage Plan (If Needed)

- If you need more space, click **Manage** > **Change Storage Plan.**

- iCloud offers paid plans starting at 50GB for $0.99 per month, which is plenty for most users.

- It's like renting a bigger storage unit when your current one is overflowing.

Step 3: Free Up Space If You're Running Low

- Delete unnecessary files, old backups, or duplicate photos in iCloud to make room for what matters.

- To manage storage, go to **System Settings** > **Apple ID** > **iCloud** > **Manage Storage.**

A little digital decluttering goes a long way.

Recovering Deleted Photos

We've all done it—accidentally deleted a photo, then instantly regretted it. But don't worry! If you delete a photo, you have 30 days to recover it before it is gone for good.

Step 1: Open Recently Deleted

- Open the **Photos app** and click **Recently Deleted** in the **Library** section of the sidebar.

- This is like your digital recycling bin—it holds deleted photos just in case you change your mind.

Step 2: Restore a Photo

- Click the photo you want to bring back and select **Restore.**

- It will go right back to your photo library, like digging an important receipt out of the trash—except much cleaner.

Step 3: Permanently Delete Photos (If Needed)

- If you are sure you want to remove a photo forever, select it and click **Delete Permanently.**

- Just be certain—because once it is gone, it is gone. Think of it like shredding an old letter—you cannot tape it back together later.

Celebrate Your Progress

Look at everything you have accomplished. You have:

- Set up **iCloud Photos** to keep your pictures backed up and accessible.

- Synced your **iPhone, iPad, and MacBook** so your photos appear everywhere.

- Learned how to **free up storage space** so you never run out of room.

- Mastered how to **recover accidentally deleted photos** just in case.

Each of these steps helps you protect and enjoy your memories without the hassle of manually saving everything. The best part? Once iCloud is set up, it runs automatically, so you don't have to do a thing.

Essential Apps for Everyday Use

DIGITAL GRANDSON PRESS

Navigating the Web with Safari

Your Simple Guide to Browsing, Bookmarking, and Staying Safe Online

The internet is an incredible place, full of information, entertainment, and ways to stay connected with the people you love. Whether you're **reading the news, searching for a new recipe, or video chatting with family**, Safari makes it easy to explore.

If the internet is a vast, open highway, **Safari is your car**—helping you get where you need to go, quickly and safely. In this chapter, we'll go over **how to browse the web, use tabs and bookmarks, adjust privacy settings, and troubleshoot common issues** so you can browse with confidence.

Getting to Know Safari

Safari is Apple's built-in web browser, and it's designed to be **simple, secure, and easy to use**. Let's start by opening it up:

- Click the **Safari icon** in your Dock—it looks like a blue compass.

- A new Safari window will open, either with a homepage or a blank window, depending on your settings.

- At the top of the screen, you'll see the **address bar**—this is where you type website addresses or search for something online.

Think of the **address bar** like a GPS—you type in a destination, and Safari takes you there.

Below the address bar, you'll see a **toolbar** with a few useful icons:

- **Back and Forward Buttons**: Click these to go back to the previous page or forward to a page you just visited.

- **Refresh Button**: Click this to reload a webpage if it isn't working properly.

That's it! **Browsing the web is as simple as typing what you want to find and pressing Return.**

Using Tabs and Bookmarks for Easy Browsing

When you're online, you may want to **view multiple websites at once**—for example, checking your email while reading an article. **Tabs** make this easy by allowing you to open several pages in the same Safari window.

Opening and Managing Tabs

- To **open a new tab**, click the **plus (+) button** next to your current tab or press **Command + T.**

- To **switch between tabs,** simply click the one you want to view.

- To **close a tab**, click the **X on the right side** of the tab or press **Command + W.**

If you **accidentally close a tab,** don't worry! Press **Command + Shift + T** to reopen it.

Saving Websites with Bookmarks

If you find a website you love and want to revisit it later, **you can save it as a bookmark**—just like marking a page in a book.

- Click the **Share icon** (a square with an arrow pointing up) and select **Add Bookmark**.

- You can also press **Command + D** as a shortcut.

- When saving a bookmark, Safari will ask where you'd like to store it.

Organizing Bookmarks for Easy Access

- To keep your bookmarks organized, use **folders**.

- Click **Bookmarks** in the top menu, then select **Add Bookmark Folder**.

- You can create folders like **Recipes, News, or Travel**—whatever makes sense for you.

Using the Favorites Bar for Quick Access

For websites you visit **frequently**, you can **add them to the Favorites Bar** so they're always just one click away.

- Drag a bookmark up to the bar beneath the address bar.

- Now, any time you want to visit that site, just click the shortcut in your Favorites Bar.

This is like **keeping your favorite book on the top shelf, always within reach**.

Keeping Your Browsing Private and Secure

The internet is a wonderful place, but it's important to **stay safe while browsing**. Safari has **built-in security features** to protect your information and privacy.

Using Private Browsing Mode

If you ever want to browse without saving your history—such as when shopping for a surprise gift—you can use **Private Browsing Mode**.

- Click **File** in the top menu and select **New Private Window**.

- The window will turn darker, meaning Safari won't save your search history or website data.

Think of it like **going incognito**—you can browse freely without leaving a trace.

Enabling Fraudulent Website Warnings

Safari can warn you if you're about to visit a **suspicious website**.

- Go to **Safari > Settings (or Preferences on macOS Monterey and earlier) > Security**.

- Make sure **Fraudulent Website Warning** is turned on.

This acts like a **guard at the door**, stopping you before you accidentally enter a risky site.

Blocking Website Tracking

Some websites **track your browsing habits** to show you targeted ads. If you want to limit this, Safari has a setting called **Intelligent Tracking Prevention**.

- Go to **Safari > Settings (or Preferences) > Privacy**.

- Check the box for **Prevent cross-site tracking**.

This is like **putting up a privacy fence** around your yard—keeping unwanted eyes out.

Troubleshooting Common Safari Issues

Even with a well-designed browser like Safari, you might run into small hiccups. Here are a few quick fixes for common issues.

1. A Webpage Won't Load

- Click the **Refresh** button (a circular arrow next to the address bar).

- If that doesn't work, check your **Wi-Fi connection** and try turning it off and back on.

Sometimes, the simplest solutions—like **restarting your router**—can fix the problem.

2. A Website Looks Strange or Won't Update

If a website isn't displaying correctly, **clearing your cache** might help.

- Go to **Safari > Settings (Preferences) > Privacy**.

- Click **Manage Website Data > Remove All** to delete stored website information.

Think of this like **cleaning out an old drawer**—sometimes, you need to clear things out to make room for new information.

3. Safari is Running Slowly

- **Close any tabs** you're not using. Having too many open at once can slow things down.

- **Clear your cache** as explained above.

- Restart Safari or, if needed, **restart your MacBook** to give it a fresh start.

This is like **decluttering your desk—when there's less mess, everything runs smoother**.

4. Updating Safari

If you're still having issues, Safari may need an update.

- On macOS Ventura and later: Go to **Apple menu** > **System Settings** > **General** > **Software Update**.

- On macOS Monterey and earlier: Go to **Apple menu** > **System Preferences** > **Software Update**.

Keeping Safari up to date ensures **you have the latest security features and improvements**.

Celebrate Your Progress!

Look at everything you've learned! You now know how to:

- **Browse the web confidently** using Safari's address bar.

- **Use tabs and bookmarks** to stay organized.

- **Keep your browsing secure** with Private Browsing Mode and Fraudulent Website Warnings.

- **Troubleshoot common Safari issues** so you can browse without frustration.

Each time you open Safari, you're building confidence and getting more comfortable with the internet.

Setting Up and Using Email in the Mail App

Sending, Organizing, and Managing Your Messages with Ease

Email is one of the best ways to stay in touch with family, friends, and businesses. Whether you're **writing to a loved one, receiving important updates, or organizing your inbox**, the Mail app on your MacBook makes it easy.

In this chapter, we'll go step by step through **setting up your email, sending messages, attaching files, and keeping your inbox organized**, so you can **spend less time sorting emails and more time enjoying them**.

Setting Up Your Email in the Mail App

Before you can start sending and receiving messages, you'll need to **connect your email account** to the Mail app. It's a **one-time setup**, and I'll guide you through it.

Opening the Mail App and Adding an Account

1. Click the **Mail app icon** in your Dock—it looks like a **blue envelope with a white paper sheet**.

2. If this is your **first time opening the app**, you'll see a setup screen right away.

3. If you've already set up another email account, you can add a new one by clicking **Mail** in the top-left menu and selecting **Add Account**.

Choosing Your Email Provider

Next, you'll be asked to select your email provider. This could be **iCloud, Gmail, Yahoo, or another service**. If you're not sure which one to pick, just **look at the part of your email address after the "@" symbol**:

- **@icloud.com** → Select **iCloud**

- **@gmail.com** → Select **Google**

- **@yahoo.com** → Select **Yahoo**

Click **Continue** and move on to the next step.

Signing In to Your Email

1. **Enter your email address and password.**

2. If you forgot your password, don't worry—it happens to all of us! Click **"Forgot password?"** and follow the instructions to reset it.

3. Once signed in, your emails will appear in the Mail app, just like letters arriving in your mailbox.

Customizing Your Notifications

If you'd like to be alerted when new emails arrive, you can **adjust your notification settings**:

- Click the **Apple menu** in the top-left corner.

- Select **System Settings** > **Notifications** > **Mail**.

- Choose how you want to be notified—by **banner, sound, or both**.

It's like deciding **whether your mail carrier rings the doorbell or just leaves the envelope in the box**—whatever works best for you.

Composing and Sending Emails

Now that your email account is set up, it's time to start sending messages!

Creating a New Email

1. Click the **New Message** button—it looks like a pencil writing on a piece of paper.

2. A new window will appear, ready for your message.

3. In the **To** field, type the recipient's email address. If they're already in your Contacts, their name will appear automatically.

Writing a Subject Line

- The **Subject** field is like the title of a letter—it tells the recipient what your email is about.

- Keep it short and clear, like **"Hello!"** or **"Question About Next Week's Plans."**

Typing Your Message

- Click in the large text area and type your email.

- If you want to **add some personality**, you can:

    ◦ **Bold or italicize words** to emphasize them.

    ◦ **Use bullet points** to list important details.

    ◦ **Add emojis** by clicking **Edit > Emoji & Symbols** in the top menu.

It's like decorating a handwritten letter—just enough to make it stand out **without going overboard**.

Attaching Photos or Documents

Want to include a **photo or file** in your email?

- Click the **paperclip icon**, choose your file, and attach it.

- This is like **putting a picture inside an envelope before mailing it**—a great way to share memories or important documents.

Adding a Clickable Link

If you'd like to **share a website**, instead of pasting a long web address, you can **turn words into a clickable link**:

- Highlight the text you want to link.

- Click **Edit > Add Link** and paste the web address.

- Now, the recipient can just **click the words** to visit the site!

Sending Your Email

Once your email is ready:

- Click the **Send** button (a paper airplane icon).

- Your message will **fly across the internet** to its destination!

Made a mistake? If your email provider allows it, you might see an **Undo Send** option at the bottom of the screen—click it quickly to **stop the email before it goes out**.

Organizing Your Inbox with Folders

A well-organized inbox makes it **easier to find important messages**. The Mail app lets you **create folders (also called "Mailboxes")** to sort emails into categories.

Creating a Folder

1. In the Mail app's left-hand sidebar, right-click **On My Mac**.

2. Select **New Mailbox** and give it a name like **Family, Bills, or Travel Plans**.

3. Click **OK**, and your new folder will appear!

It's like **labeling a file folder** so everything stays neat and easy to find.

Moving Emails into Folders

- **Drag and drop** an email into a folder to organize it.

- Think of it as **placing a letter into the correct drawer**—now you'll always know where to find it.

Using Rules to Sort Emails Automatically

If you receive a lot of emails, you can set **Rules** to **automatically organize them**:

- Click **Mail > Settings (or Preferences) > Rules**.

- Click **Add Rule** and set conditions like **"Move all emails from Sarah into my Family folder."**

Now, your MacBook **sorts your mail for you**, just like a helpful assistant.

Archiving Emails to Declutter Your Inbox

If you want to save emails but **don't need them in your inbox**, you can **archive them**:

- Click **Archive** to move them out of sight while keeping them accessible.

- It's like **putting old letters in a storage box**—safe, but out of the way.

Finding Emails Quickly with Search & Filters

Can't find an email? No problem—Mail has **search tools** to help.

Using the Search Bar

1. Click the **search bar** at the top of the Mail window.

2. Type a keyword, such as the sender's name or part of the subject line.

3. Mail will show you all the matching emails—like **digging through a stack of letters and instantly pulling out the one you need**.

Narrowing Down Your Search

If you have too many results:

- Click **From, To, or Subject** under the search bar to focus your search.

Filtering Your Inbox

You can **temporarily hide emails** to focus on what matters:

- Click the **Filter icon** and choose **Unread Messages, Attachments, or Flagged Messages**.

- It's like **sorting mail into different piles**—urgent on top, everything else for later.

Using Smart Mailboxes for Auto-Sorting

Want Mail to group emails for you?

- Click **Mailbox > New Smart Mailbox**.

- Set rules like **"Show all emails from last week"** or **"Only emails with attachments."**

Now, Mail **organizes your inbox for you**, making everything easy to find.

You've Got Mail... and You're in Control!

Look at everything you've learned! You can now **send, organize, and manage emails** with ease. Whether you're keeping in touch with family or handling important documents, you **have the tools to stay organized and connected**.

Enjoy your email—and remember, you're doing a fantastic job! Keep practicing, keep exploring, and most of all, **have fun staying in touch with the people who matter most!**

Staying Connected: Using FaceTime and Messages on Your MacBook

Video Calls, Texting, and Sharing with Loved Ones

Few things are better than seeing a loved one's face, even if they're miles away. Whether you're checking in on family, catching up with friends, or sharing exciting news, FaceTime makes video calling easy. And when a quick message will do, the Messages app lets you send texts, photos, and more—right from your MacBook. Let's set everything up so you can start connecting with confidence.

Setting Up FaceTime for Video Calls

Before making your first FaceTime call, let's get everything ready.

Open FaceTime and Sign In

Click the **FaceTime** icon in your Dock—it looks like a green video camera. If you don't see it, press **Command + Spacebar**, type "FaceTime," and press **Return** to open it.

The first time you use FaceTime, you'll need to sign in with your **Apple ID**. If you've already set up an Apple ID, enter your email address and password. If you don't remember your login details, click **Forgot Apple ID or Password?** and follow the steps to reset it.

Check Your FaceTime Settings

Before making your first call, take a moment to customize your FaceTime settings. Click **FaceTime** in the top menu bar, then select **Settings**. Here, you can:

- Choose which **phone number or email address** people can use to reach you.

- Make sure **FaceTime is enabled** (the toggle switch should be turned on).

- Decide whether to allow **Live Photos** to be taken during a call.

Once that's set, you're ready to make your first call!

Adding and Managing Contacts

To make FaceTime calls or send messages, you'll need contacts stored on your MacBook.

Add a Contact in the Contacts App

Click the **Contacts** app in your Dock—it looks like an address book. If you don't see it, use **Command + Spacebar** and type "Contacts" to find it.

1. Click the + button at the bottom of the window.

2. Select **New Contact** and enter the person's **name, phone number, and email**.

3. Click **Done** to save them.

Once a contact is saved, they'll automatically show up in FaceTime and Messages, making it easy to reach them.

Quickly Call Someone Without Adding Them

If you haven't added someone to your contacts yet, that's okay! Just open Face-Time and type their **email address or phone number** into the search bar. Click their name, then select **Video** or **Audio** to start the call.

Save Favorites for Easy Access

If you frequently call someone, add them to your **Favorites** for quick access. In FaceTime, click the **Info (i)** button next to their name, then select **Add to Favorites**.

Making and Receiving FaceTime Calls

Start a FaceTime Call

1. Open **FaceTime**.

2. Type the **name, phone number, or email** of the person you want to call.

3. Click **Video** for a video call or **Audio** for a voice-only call.

If the person is saved in your **Favorites**, you can just click their name and start the call immediately.

Answer an Incoming FaceTime Call

When someone calls you on FaceTime, you'll see a notification pop up. You can:

- Click **Accept** to answer the call.

- Click **Decline** if you can't talk right now.

- Click **Message** to send them a quick text instead.

If you miss a call, don't worry—you'll see it listed in the **FaceTime app** under **Recents**, so you can call them back later.

Using Messages for Texts and Photos

If you'd rather send a quick message instead of making a call, the **Messages** app is the way to go.

Open Messages and Sign In

Click the **Messages** icon in your Dock—it looks like a speech bubble. If it's not there, press **Command + Spacebar**, type "Messages," and press **Return** to open it.

The first time you use Messages, sign in with your **Apple ID**. If you're already logged into FaceTime, Messages should be set up automatically.

Start a New Conversation

1. Click the **New Message** button (a pencil inside a square).

2. In the **To** field, type the recipient's **name, phone number, or email**.

3. Type your message in the text box at the bottom, then press **Return** to send it.

Send Photos, Videos, and More

- To send a **photo or video**, click the + button next to the text box and choose **Photos**.

- To add **emojis**, click the **emoji icon** (a smiley face).

- To **react to a message**, right-click it and choose **Tapback** (a thumbs-up, heart, etc.).

Group Messages

To message multiple people at once, just add more names in the **To** field. Everyone in the group will see the conversation, just like a shared text thread on your phone.

Share Your Location

If you're meeting up with someone, you can share your location. Click **Details** in the top-right corner of a conversation, then select **Send My Current Location**.

Troubleshooting FaceTime and Messages

Even with the best technology, things don't always go as planned. Here are some quick solutions if something isn't working:

FaceTime Isn't Connecting

- Make sure your **Wi-Fi is turned on** and you're connected to the internet.

- Restart FaceTime by going to **FaceTime > Settings** and toggling FaceTime **off and on**.

- Try **restarting your MacBook**—sometimes a fresh start fixes small glitches.

Messages Won't Send

- Make sure you're **signed in** to your Apple ID under **Messages > Settings > iMessage**.

- Check your internet connection—Messages needs Wi-Fi or an internet connection to work.

- If you're trying to message someone who doesn't have an iPhone, make sure **Send as SMS** is enabled in Settings.

Can't Hear or See Someone on FaceTime?

- Check that your **microphone and camera** are enabled in **System Settings > Privacy & Security**.

- If the video is blurry, move closer to your **Wi-Fi router** for a stronger signal.

- Make sure your **software is up to date** under **System Settings > Software Update**.

Celebrate Your Progress

You've just mastered two of the most useful communication tools on your MacBook! Now, you can **call, text, and share moments** with the people who matter most—whether they're across the street or across the country.

The more you use FaceTime and Messages, the more natural it will feel. If something doesn't go right the first time, that's okay—just try again. The important thing is that **you're learning, exploring, and staying connected**.

Enjoy catching up with loved ones, sending quick notes, and making video calls with confidence. **You've got this!**

MASTERING EVENTS AND REMINDERS ON YOUR MACBOOK

STAY ORGANIZED WITH THE CALENDAR AND REMINDERS APPS

Your MacBook makes it easy to stay on top of important dates, whether it's a doctor's appointment, a family gathering, or a daily reminder to take your medication. The **Calendar** and **Reminders** apps work together to help you manage your schedule, keep track of to-do lists, and ensure you never miss a thing. Let's go step by step to set them up and make them work for you.

Setting Up Events in the Calendar App

The **Calendar app** is your digital planner, allowing you to schedule events, set reminders, and even share your schedule with family members.

Opening the Calendar App
Click the **Calendar** icon in your Dock—it looks like a small monthly calendar. When you open it, today's date will be highlighted. Think of this as your personal command center for all upcoming events.

Adding a New Event

1. **Double-click** on the day you want to schedule something. A new event window will pop up.

2. Enter a title, such as "Lunch with Sarah."

3. Choose a **time and location** if needed. If you're meeting at a restaurant, typing in the name may even bring up a map preview.

4. Add any **notes** or details, like "Bring Sarah's favorite cookies!"

Setting Event Alerts

To make sure you don't forget, add an **alert** that reminds you ahead of time. Click the **Alert** dropdown and select a time, whether it's 10 minutes before or a full day in advance. If the event is really important, set **multiple** reminders so you have plenty of notice.

Recurring Events

If you have a regular appointment—like a weekly fitness class or a monthly book club—set it up once and let Calendar handle the rest. Click the **Repeat** option and select **daily, weekly, monthly, or yearly.** Now, it will automatically appear on your calendar every time without you having to re-enter it.

Using the Reminders App to Stay on Track

The **Reminders app** is perfect for tasks that don't have a set time, like watering the plants, picking up groceries, or taking your medication.

Opening the Reminders App

Click the **Reminders** icon in your Dock, which looks like a checklist. This app allows you to create simple reminders and to-do lists that help you manage daily tasks.

Creating a Reminder

1. Click **New Reminder** and type in what you need to remember, like "Buy milk."

2. If you want a specific **date and time**, click the **i** (information) button and select **Remind me on a day** to choose when the alert should go off.

3. You can also set **location-based reminders**, like "Remind me to pick up dry cleaning when I leave the house." Your MacBook will use your iPhone's location to send the alert at the right time.

Organizing Reminders into Lists

To stay even more organized, create separate lists for different types of tasks.

- Click **Add List** and name it something useful, like **Groceries, Work Tasks, or Chores.**

- You can also **color-code lists** to make them easier to recognize at a glance.

- To move reminders between lists, just **drag and drop** them.

Syncing Events and Reminders Across Your Devices

One of the best parts of using your MacBook's Calendar and Reminders apps is that they **sync across all your Apple devices**. If you add an event on your MacBook, it will show up on your iPhone or iPad, so you always have your schedule with you.

Turning on iCloud Sync

1. Click the **Apple** icon in the top-left corner and go to **System Settings.**

2. Click **Apple ID**, then select **iCloud.**

3. Make sure **Calendars** and **Reminders** are turned on.

Once iCloud is enabled, any event or reminder you create will automatically appear on all of your Apple devices—no need to manually enter the same information twice.

Adding Events from Your iPhone

If you create an event on your iPhone, it will show up on your MacBook instantly. This makes it easy to schedule plans on the go and then view them later on a bigger screen.

Using Handoff to Switch Devices Seamlessly

Handoff lets you start an event or reminder on one Apple device and finish it on another. If you begin adding a calendar event on your iPhone, your MacBook will show an **icon in the Dock** that lets you pick up right where you left off.

Sharing Your Calendar with Family

If you want to keep your family on the same page, you can **share a calendar** with them.

- Open **Calendar** and **right-click** on a calendar in the left-hand sidebar.

- Select **Share Calendar** and enter the email addresses of family members you want to include.

Now, they'll be able to see and add events, helping everyone stay in sync with birthdays, vacations, and family plans.

Customizing Notifications and Alerts

To make sure you never miss an important date, you can **customize your alerts** in **System Settings.**

1. Click the **Apple** icon and select **System Settings.**

2. Choose **Notifications.**

3. Select **Calendar** or **Reminders** and adjust the alert style. You can choose between:

- **Banners** (which disappear after a moment)

- **Alerts** (which stay on-screen until you dismiss them)

- **Sounds** to accompany your reminders

If you tend to get distracted, setting **multiple alerts** can help reinforce an important task.

Snoozing Alerts
If an alert pops up but you need more time, you can **snooze** it for later. Simply click **Snooze**, and the reminder will return in a few minutes.

Default Alerts for All Events
If you prefer to always receive reminders **a day before an event**, you can set this as a default:

- Open **Calendar** and go to **Preferences.**

- Click **Alerts** and set your preferred reminder time.

This way, every new event will automatically include an alert without you having to add one manually.

Tips for Staying Organized

- **Color-Code Events** – Assign colors to different types of events so you can quickly see what's coming up.

- **Create Multiple Calendars** – Have separate calendars for work, personal events, and family plans to keep things neat.

- **Use Notes and Attachments** – Add important details like addresses, instructions, or PDF attachments to events.

- **Check Your Calendar Daily** – Take a minute each morning to review what's ahead, so you're always prepared.

- **Use Siri for Quick Reminders** – Just say, "Hey Siri, remind me to call John at 3 PM," and Siri will take care of the rest.

Celebrate Your Progress

You've just set up two of the most powerful organizational tools on your MacBook. The **Calendar and Reminders apps** are designed to simplify your life by keeping all of your important dates and tasks in one place.

With a little practice, managing your schedule will become second nature. Whether it's remembering an anniversary, scheduling an appointment, or planning a family gathering, these tools will help keep you on track.

You're doing an amazing job—keep going!

Turning Your MacBook into an Entertainment Hub

Books, Music, and Games at Your Fingertips

Your MacBook isn't just for emails and organizing files—it's also a fantastic way to unwind, explore new interests, and have a little fun. Whether you love reading a good book, listening to your favorite music, or playing games to relax, your MacBook has plenty of ways to bring entertainment into your day.

Let's walk through some of the best apps for books, music, and games—and how to download them so you can enjoy everything your MacBook has to offer.

Turning Your MacBook Into a Digital Bookshelf

If you love getting lost in a good book, your MacBook can become your personal library—without the need for extra shelf space! With the right apps, you can browse thousands of books, adjust the text size for comfortable reading, and even listen to audiobooks.

Here are some of the best reading apps you can download from the App Store:

- **Apple Books** – Already built into your MacBook, Apple Books offers a vast selection of books, from bestsellers to classic literature. It's like stepping into your favorite bookstore, but without leaving your chair. You can change the text size, highlight passages, and even take notes as you read.

- **Kindle** – If you've ever used an Amazon Kindle, you'll feel right at home with this app. The Kindle app syncs your books across all your devices, so you can start a book on your MacBook and continue reading on your iPhone or iPad—just like carrying a bookmark that follows you everywhere.

- **Audible** – Prefer listening instead of reading? Audible lets you enjoy audiobooks read by professional narrators. It's like having a storyteller in your pocket, ready to read to you anytime you like. Perfect for multi-tasking or winding down at the end of the day.

Streaming Music on Your MacBook

Music can set the mood for anything—whether you're relaxing, working, or just enjoying your morning coffee. Your MacBook makes it easy to stream music with these popular apps:

- **Apple Music** – Apple's built-in music streaming service gives you access to millions of songs. You can create playlists, listen to live radio, and even explore hand-picked recommendations based on your tastes. It's like having every record store you've ever loved right at your fingertips.

- **Spotify** – Known for its incredible playlist suggestions, Spotify is great for discovering new music. Whether you need an upbeat playlist for your morning walk or something calming before bed, Spotify has a mix ready for every moment. It's like having a friend who always knows the perfect song to play.

- **Pandora** – If you like to be surprised, Pandora creates personalized radio stations based on your favorite songs and artists. Over time, it learns your preferences—like a DJ who gets better at reading the room with every song.

You can listen to all of these apps using your MacBook's built-in speakers or connect Bluetooth headphones for a more private experience.

Finding Games for Relaxation and Fun

Your MacBook is also a great way to unwind with a fun game. Whether you enjoy solving puzzles, playing card games, or exploring new worlds, there's something for everyone in the App Store.

- **Word and Puzzle Games** – If you love crosswords or brain teasers, apps like Wordscapes and Sudoku will keep your mind sharp while you relax.

- **Classic Card and Board Games** – Prefer something more familiar? You can find digital versions of games like Solitaire, Chess, and Mahjong to enjoy at your own pace.

- **Adventure and Strategy Games** – If you like a little more excitement, there are adventure and strategy games that let you explore, solve mysteries, and build virtual worlds.

Think of the App Store as an arcade—you can browse, try out new games, and find ones that suit your style without spending a fortune.

How to Download Apps from the App Store

Now that you know about some great apps, let's get them onto your MacBook!

1. **Open the App Store** – Click the App Store icon in your Dock (it looks like a blue circle with a capital "A"). This is where you'll find new apps, just like a digital shopping mall for software.

2. **Search for an App** – Use the search bar in the top-right corner to type in the name of the app you want (such as "Spotify" or "Kindle"). If you're not sure what to look for, you can browse through different categories.

3. **Click Install** – When you find an app you like, click the **Get** or **Install** button. If the app isn't free, you'll see the price listed instead. You may need to enter your Apple ID password for security.

4. **Find Your New App** – Once installed, you'll find your app in **Launchpad** (the icon in your Dock with a grid of small circles). From there, just click the app to open it and start exploring.

Enjoying Your Personalized Entertainment Hub

You've just unlocked a whole new side of your MacBook—one filled with books, music, and games to brighten your day. Whether you're reading a new novel, listening to your favorite playlist, or playing a relaxing game, your MacBook is now your personal entertainment center.

Take your time exploring new apps and trying different features. The more you use them, the more comfortable and enjoyable they'll become. If you ever feel stuck, just refer back to this guide—or better yet, ask Siri for help!

You're doing an amazing job, and I hope you have fun making your MacBook truly your own. Now, go ahead and play that song you love, dive into a new book, or challenge yourself with a fun game—you deserve it!

Keyboard Shortcuts to Save Time

DIGITAL GRANDSON PRESS

MASTERING MACBOOK SHORTCUTS: SIMPLE TRICKS TO SAVE YOU TIME

SPEED UP EVERYDAY TASKS WITH THESE EASY KEYBOARD COMMANDS

Your MacBook's keyboard isn't just for typing—it's a powerful tool that can help you navigate, edit, and organize with ease. Think of keyboard shortcuts like secret handshakes: once you know them, they make everything faster and smoother. Instead of clicking through menus or dragging your mouse all over the screen, these simple key combinations will help you get things done effortlessly.

At first, shortcuts may feel a little tricky—kind of like learning where all the light switches are in a new house. But with a little practice, they'll become second nature, and you'll wonder how you ever used your MacBook without them. Let's dive in!

Essential Shortcuts for Editing Text

If you spend time writing emails, taking notes, or organizing documents, these shortcuts will quickly become your best friends. They'll save you from unnecessary clicking and make editing a breeze.

- **Copy (Command + C):** Copies selected text or images so you can use them elsewhere. Think of it like using a recipe card—you still have the original, but now you have an extra copy to share.

- **Paste (Command + V):** Inserts whatever you've copied into a new location. Like taking that extra recipe card and putting it in a new cookbook.

- **Cut (Command + X):** Removes selected text or images but keeps them saved in memory until you paste them. Imagine moving a sticky note from one page to another instead of rewriting it.

- **Undo (Command + Z):** A lifesaver! This instantly erases your last action. Accidentally deleted a sentence? One tap and it's back, like rewinding time.

- **Redo (Command + Shift + Z):** If you undo something and change your mind, redo brings it back. Like deciding you actually *did* want that last slice of cake after all.

These shortcuts aren't just about speed—they reduce frustration, especially when fixing small mistakes. The more you use them, the more automatic they'll become!

Navigating Your MacBook with Keyboard Commands

Sometimes, switching between apps or finding files with your trackpad can feel like searching for your reading glasses—there's a faster way! These shortcuts help you zip around your MacBook without breaking your flow.

- **Spotlight Search (Command + Space):** Need to find a document, app, or even a website? Press Command + Space to open Spotlight, then start typing. It's like having a personal assistant who instantly fetches what you need.

- **Switch Between Apps (Command + Tab):** If you're jumping between your email and a web page, hold Command and tap Tab to switch back and forth. Like flipping between channels on TV without needing the remote.

- **Open a New Finder Window (Command + N):** While in Finder, press this shortcut to open another window. Perfect for moving files between folders, like opening a second drawer in a filing cabinet.

Once you get used to these, you'll find yourself zipping around your MacBook with confidence.

Managing Files with Finder Shortcuts

The Finder is like your digital filing cabinet. These shortcuts make it easier to keep everything neat and organized.

- **New Folder (Command + Shift + N):** Creates a new folder instantly. It's like grabbing a fresh file folder to store important papers.

- **Delete File (Command + Delete):** Moves a selected file to the trash—no need to drag it. Like crumpling up a piece of paper and tossing it in the bin.

- **Select All (Command + A):** Selects everything in a folder, perfect for moving or deleting multiple files at once. Like scooping up a whole pile of papers in one motion.

- **Quick Look (Spacebar):** Want to peek at a file without opening it? Select it and press the spacebar. It's like flipping open a book to glance at the first page before deciding to read it.

Organizing files is one of the best ways to keep your MacBook running smoothly. These shortcuts make it quick and easy!

Practice Makes Perfect: Try These Shortcuts Today

The best way to master keyboard shortcuts is to practice them in real situations. Here are a few fun ways to try them out:

- **Write Yourself a Note:** Open the Notes app and type a quick message. Use Command + C to copy it, then Command + V to paste it in another note. Try undoing a sentence (Command + Z), then redoing it (Command + Shift + Z).

- **Organize Your Desktop:** Use Command + Shift + N to create new folders, then drag files into them. Press Command + Delete to clean up any unnecessary items.

- **Search for a File:** Press Command + Space and type the name of a document or app you want to open—watch how quickly Spotlight finds it for you!

- **Switch Between Apps:** Open a couple of apps and use Command + Tab to cycle between them without touching the trackpad.

The more you use these shortcuts, the more second nature they'll become.

Celebrate Your Progress!

Look at you go! Learning keyboard shortcuts is like unlocking a hidden superpower on your MacBook. At first, it might feel like learning a new language, but soon, you'll be zipping through tasks effortlessly.

Try to incorporate one or two new shortcuts into your daily routine, and before you know it, they'll be muscle memory. You're doing a fantastic job, and every time you use a shortcut instead of clicking through menus, you're making your MacBook work *for* you instead of the other way around.

Keep up the great work—you've got this!

MASTERING MULTITASKING: ADVANCED KEYBOARD SHORTCUTS

SPEED UP YOUR WORKFLOW AND STAY ORGANIZED ON YOUR MACBOOK

By now, you've learned the basics of keyboard shortcuts, but why stop there? Once you get comfortable, these shortcuts can help you *really* take control of your MacBook. Whether you're switching between apps, setting up custom shortcuts, or managing multiple windows at once, these advanced tricks will save you time and frustration.

Think of it like learning to drive a car. At first, you're just figuring out how to steer and use the brakes. But once you're comfortable, you start using shortcuts—adjusting your mirrors quickly, using cruise control, or parallel parking with ease. These MacBook shortcuts work the same way: they make everything smoother, faster, and more efficient.

Let's dive in!

Quickly Switch Between Open Apps

If you've ever found yourself clicking around, trying to find the app you *swore* was just open, this section is for you. Instead of hunting through windows, try these shortcuts:

- **Switch Between Apps (Command + Tab)** – Hold Command and tap Tab to cycle through all your open apps. Keep holding Command while tapping Tab to move through them, then release when you land on the one you need. It's like flipping through a magazine until you find the page you want—but much faster.

- **Switch Between Windows of the Same App (Command +)** – Let's say you have multiple Safari windows open. Instead of hunting for the right one, press Command + (the little key above Tab) to flip through them quickly. No more digging through a cluttered desktop!

- **See All Open Windows at Once (Control + Up Arrow)** – Press Control + Up Arrow to launch Mission Control, which spreads out all your open apps so you can see everything at a glance. Think of it as laying out all your papers on a desk so you can grab exactly what you need.

Once you get used to these shortcuts, switching between apps will feel effortless—like muscle memory.

Multitasking Made Easy

If you're juggling multiple tasks—whether it's keeping an email open while checking your calendar or writing notes while watching a video—these multitasking features will help you stay on track.

- **Split View for Side-by-Side Apps** – Instead of constantly switching back and forth, you can have two apps open side by side. Here's how:

  a. Click and hold the green button in the top-left corner of a window.

  b. Select "Tile Window to Left" or "Tile Window to Right."

  c. Choose the second app you want to view.

- **App Exposé (Control + Down Arrow)** – If you're working within an app that has multiple windows open, press Control + Down Arrow to see all its open windows at once. This is especially useful in Safari, Mail, or Word when you have multiple documents or web pages open.

- **Hot Corners for Quick Actions** – Hot Corners let you trigger an action just by moving your cursor to a screen corner. You can set one corner to open Mission Control, another to show the desktop, and so on. To set them up:

  a. Open System Settings.

  b. Click **Desktop & Dock** (in the sidebar).

  c. Scroll down and click **Hot Corners** to customize.

Create Your Own Keyboard Shortcuts

MacBooks come with plenty of built-in shortcuts, but did you know you can create your own? If there's a task you do frequently—like opening your favorite note-taking app—you can set up a shortcut that works just for you.

Here's how to create a custom shortcut:

1. Open **System Settings** and click **Keyboard** in the sidebar.

2. Select **Keyboard Shortcuts.**

3. Choose **App Shortcuts** and click + to add a new one.

4. Enter the menu command exactly as it appears in the app (for example, "Save As...").

5. Assign your custom shortcut using a key combination.

Now, instead of hunting through menus, you can perform the action with a quick keystroke.

Troubleshooting Shortcuts That Don't Work

If a shortcut isn't working, don't worry—there's usually a simple fix. Here are some common issues and solutions:

- **The Shortcut Is Conflicting with Another One** – If a shortcut isn't responding, check **System Settings > Keyboard > Keyboard Shortcuts** to see if another function is using the same key combination. Adjust it if necessary.

- **The Shortcut Only Works in Certain Apps** – Some shortcuts, like Command + ` (switching between windows), only work within a single app. If a shortcut isn't behaving as expected, double-check that it's meant to work in that specific app.

- **Reset Keyboard Shortcuts** – If shortcuts are acting up, you can restore them to default settings:

  a. Go to **System Settings > Keyboard > Keyboard Shortcuts**

  b. Click **Restore Defaults.**

It's like pressing the reset button on a tricky puzzle—sometimes starting fresh is the best solution!

Celebrate Your Progress

Look at you go! You've learned how to move between apps like a pro, multitask with ease, and even create your own custom shortcuts. At first, remembering these shortcuts might feel like learning a new dance—your fingers may hesitate.

But with practice, they'll become second nature, and you'll wonder how you ever lived without them.

Keep practicing, have fun experimenting, and don't be afraid to try new short-cuts. The more you use them, the more confident and in control you'll feel. You've got this!

CUSTOMIZING KEYBOARD SHORTCUTS

MAKE YOUR MACBOOK WORK FOR YOU

Shortcuts aren't just about saving time—they're about making your MacBook work **exactly** the way you want it to. Think of it like arranging your kitchen: when everything is set up **just right**, you don't have to dig through drawers to find what you need. The same goes for your MacBook. By customizing keyboard shortcuts, you can simplify your most-used tasks and make navigating your computer feel effortless.

In this chapter, we'll go over how to access your keyboard shortcut settings, create your own custom shortcuts, and manage the ones you already have. Whether you're opening your favorite apps, switching between tools, or organizing files, the right shortcuts can make everything smoother. Let's dive in!

Accessing the Keyboard Shortcuts Menu

Before we start customizing, let's find where all the shortcuts live. Think of this as opening your toolbox before you start a project.

To Open Keyboard Settings:

1. Press **Command + Spacebar** to open **Spotlight Search**

2. Type **Keyboard** and press **Return**

3. Select the **Keyboard Shortcuts** tab

Here, you'll see a list of **categories** like **Mission Control**, **Screenshots**, and **App Shortcuts**. This is where you'll create, modify, and organize your short-cuts.

Creating Your Own Shortcuts

Custom shortcuts are like carving your own shortcut path through a park—you skip the long way around and get straight to where you need to go. If there's an action you do frequently (like opening a specific folder or creating a new email), you can make a shortcut to do it instantly.

To Add a New Shortcut:

1. Open **Keyboard Shortcuts** (using the steps above).

2. Select **App Shortcuts** from the left-hand sidebar.

3. Click the + **(plus) button** at the bottom of the window.

4. A new window will appear:

    ○ **Application**: Choose the app where you want this shortcut to work (like Safari or Mail).

    ○ **Menu Title**: Type the exact name of the command as it appears in the app's menu. (For example, if you want to create a shortcut for opening a new tab in Safari, type **"New Tab"** exactly as it appears in the menu.)

    ○ **Keyboard Shortcut**: Click this field and press the keys you want to use for your shortcut.

5. Click **Add** and test your shortcut!

Tip: Choose shortcuts that are easy to remember but not ones you'll press by accident. If you use Command + N often for "New Document," you probably don't want to assign it to something else.

Managing and Editing Shortcuts

Once you start using shortcuts, you may find that some need **tweaking** or that others **conflict with existing ones**. That's okay! Just like rearranging furniture, you can always move things around until they feel right.

To Edit or Delete a Shortcut:

1. Return to **Keyboard Shortcuts** in **System Settings**.

2. Find the shortcut you want to change.

3. Click on it, then press the new keys you want to assign.

4. To delete a shortcut, select it and click the - **(minus) button**.

Tip: If a shortcut isn't working, it might be conflicting with another one. Try checking the **category menus** in Keyboard Shortcuts to make sure no two commands are using the same keys.

Practice Your Shortcuts in Everyday Tasks

Shortcuts are most useful when they **become second nature**, so the best way to learn them is through **practice**. Here are some easy ways to build shortcut habits:

- **Write a quick note**: Open **Notes**, type something, then practice copying (Command + C), pasting (Command + V), and undoing (Command + Z).

- **Move files quickly**: Create a new folder (Command + Shift + N), move some files into it, and then delete one using Command + Delete.

- **Switch apps with ease**: Open a few apps (like Safari, Mail, and Calendar), then use **Command + Tab** to flip between them instead of clicking.

- **Preview files instantly**: Select a document or photo in Finder and press **Spacebar** to get a Quick Look preview without opening it.

The more you **intentionally** use shortcuts in your daily routine, the **faster and easier** they will feel!

Celebrate Your Progress

Look at you—customizing your MacBook like a pro! By setting up your own shortcuts, you're making your computer work exactly the way you want it to. And each time you use a shortcut instead of clicking through menus, you're saving yourself time and effort.

If some shortcuts don't stick right away, **don't stress**. Learning new habits takes time. The more you practice, the more natural they will feel. Before long, you'll be navigating your MacBook **faster than ever**—and wondering how you ever lived without these tricks!

Keep up the great work! You've got this.

Security Tips and Staying Safe Online

DIGITAL GRANDSON PRESS

KEEPING YOUR MACBOOK SAFE: SIMPLE SECURITY TIPS

PROTECTING YOUR PERSONAL INFORMATION AND STAYING SECURE ONLINE

Your MacBook holds so much of your life—family photos, important emails, favorite websites—so keeping it secure isn't just about technology, it's about **peace of mind**. Think of it like **locking your front door** or **keeping a spare key in a safe place**. With a few simple steps, you can make sure your MacBook stays protected without adding stress to your day.

In this chapter, we'll go over how to **set up a strong password, update your MacBook for better security, manage app permissions, and browse the web safely**. Let's take control of your security—one easy step at a time.

Creating a Strong Password

Your MacBook's password is like **the key to your home**—it should be **easy for you to remember, but impossible for anyone else to guess**.

Setting Up or Changing Your Password

- Press **Command + Spacebar**, type **Touch ID & Password**, and press **Return**.

- Click **Change Password** at the top of the page.

- Enter your new password and confirm it.

Choosing a Strong Password

Instead of using something simple like **"123456" or "password"** (which are surprisingly common!), try a phrase that's personal to you but hard for others to guess.

Example: GrandmaMakesTheBestApplePie42!
It's long, unique, and easy to remember!

Extra Tip: Use Touch ID for Faster, Secure Access

If your MacBook has a **Touch ID sensor** (usually on the top right of the keyboard), you can unlock your MacBook with **your fingerprint instead of typing a password**. Just turn it on in **Touch ID & Password settings**.

Keeping Your MacBook Updated

Updating your MacBook is **like getting a free security upgrade**—it keeps everything running smoothly and **protects you from new threats** without any extra effort.

How to Check for Updates

- Press **Command + Spacebar**, type **Software Update**, and press **Return**.

- If an update is available, click **Update Now**.

- To make things even easier, turn on **Automatic Updates** so your Mac-

Book stays current without you having to check.

Why does this matter? Updates don't just add new features—they **fix security gaps** that hackers try to exploit. Staying updated means **your MacBook is always at its safest**.

Managing App Permissions

Some apps **ask for access to your camera, microphone, or location**—but not every app actually needs that access. It's a good idea to **check what you've allowed** and **turn off anything unnecessary**.

How to Review App Permissions

- Press **Command + Spacebar**, type **Privacy & Security**, and press **Return**.

- Click on categories like **Camera, Microphone, and Location Services** to see which apps have access.

- If you see an app you **don't recognize or don't use**, turn **off** the switch next to it (blue = on, gray = off).

Think of it like **giving out spare keys**—only trusted people (or apps) should have access! And remember, if you ever turn off access and realize you need it later, you can always turn it back on.

Safe and Secure Web Browsing

The internet is **a fantastic place**, but it's important to **stay cautious while browsing**—just like exploring a new city, you want to **be aware of your surroundings**.

Using Safari's Built-in Privacy Features

Safari has **strong privacy tools** to keep you safe while browsing:

- Open **Safari**, click **Safari** in the top menu, then choose **Settings > Privacy**.

- Turn on **Prevent Cross-Site Tracking**—this stops websites from following you across the internet.

- Click **About Safari & Privacy** to learn more about built-in security protections.

How to Spot and Avoid Suspicious Links

- **Be cautious with unexpected emails**—if you don't recognize the sender or it sounds **too good to be true**, don't click any links.

- **Check the website address**—if you're on a banking or shopping site, make sure the URL starts with **"https://"** (the "s" stands for secure).

- **Don't enter personal info on pop-ups**—legitimate companies won't ask for passwords or credit card details this way.

Turn on Private Browsing for Extra Privacy

If you're using a shared computer or just want **extra privacy**, you can browse in **Private Mode**:

- In Safari, click **File > New Private Window**.

- This prevents Safari from **saving your browsing history** and stops websites from tracking your activity.

Browsing safely is **all about awareness**—if something feels off, **trust your instincts and steer clear**.

Celebrate Your Progress!

Look at you—**taking control of your MacBook's security like a pro!** You've learned how to:

- **Create a strong, secure password** that's easy to remember.

- **Keep your MacBook updated** to stay protected.

- **Manage app permissions** so only trusted apps have access.

- **Browse safely online** by avoiding suspicious links and using Safari's privacy settings.

These small changes **make a big difference** in keeping your MacBook safe and **giving you peace of mind**. If you ever feel unsure, remember—you're learning something new every day, and you've got this!

STAYING SAFE ONLINE

HOW TO SPOT SCAMS AND PROTECT YOUR PERSONAL INFO

The internet is an amazing place—it helps you stay connected, learn new things, and even manage your daily life. But just like in the real world, there are people out there trying to take advantage of others. That's why learning to recognize online scams is so important.

Think of it like this: You wouldn't give your house keys to a stranger just because they claim to be from the electric company. The same rule applies online—if someone you don't know is asking for personal information, you should always be skeptical.

In this chapter, I'll show you how to **spot phishing scams, avoid online fraud, report suspicious activity, and use security tools to keep your MacBook safe.** Let's get started!

How to Recognize Phishing Emails and Text Messages

Ever get an email or text that just feels... off? Maybe it claims to be from your bank, a shipping company, or even a friend in distress, asking you to click a link or provide personal information. That's called **phishing**—a scam where cybercriminals pretend to be someone trustworthy to steal your info.

Here's how to **spot** and **avoid** phishing attempts:

- **Check the Sender's Email Address** – Scammers try to mimic real companies, but their email addresses often look strange. If your bank normally emails you from "support@yourbank.com" but you get a message from "customer-service-123@randomsite.com," that's a big red flag.

- **Look for Spelling and Grammar Mistakes** – Legitimate companies proofread their emails. If something reads like it was written in a rush (or by someone who failed English class), be suspicious.

- **Beware of Urgent Requests** – If an email claims your account will be "locked immediately" unless you click a link, don't panic. Scammers **want** you to act fast so you don't have time to think.

- **Don't Click on Links** – Instead of clicking, open your web browser and go directly to the company's official website to check for alerts. If it's a real issue, you'll see it there.

- **Never Share Personal Information Over Email or Text** – Banks, government agencies, and real businesses **will never** ask for sensitive information this way. If in doubt, call the company directly using a trusted phone number.

Bottom line: If something feels off, trust your gut! It's better to double-check than to fall for a scam.

Avoiding Common Online Scams

Scammers are always coming up with new tricks, but most scams follow a **few predictable patterns.** Here are some of the most common ones and how to avoid them:

"You've Won a Prize!" Scams

You get an email, text, or pop-up that says you've won **a free vacation, a new iPhone, or a million dollars**—all you have to do is "click here" or pay a small fee to claim your prize.

Reality check: If you didn't enter a contest, you didn't win a contest! No one is giving away expensive prizes for free.

Tech Support Scams

A scary pop-up appears on your screen saying **"Your computer is infected! Call this number for help."** These scammers pose as Apple or Microsoft support, then try to convince you to give them remote access to your MacBook.

Reality check: Apple will NEVER send pop-ups like this or ask you to call them for "urgent tech support." If you see a message like this, close the pop-up and run a trusted security scan instead.

Fake Charity Scams

Scammers take advantage of people's generosity by posing as charities—especially during **natural disasters or world events.** They'll ask for donations, but the money goes straight into their pockets.

Reality check: Always research charities before donating. Visit their official website directly or use a trusted site like **Charity Navigator** to verify them.

Rule of thumb: If something seems **too good to be true, it probably is!** Always take a step back and think before clicking, donating, or sharing personal info.

Reporting Suspicious Activity

If you come across a scam or phishing attempt, reporting it helps protect not just you, but others too. Here's what to do:

- **Report Phishing Emails** – If you get a fake email from a company, forward it to their official fraud department. (For example, Apple accepts reports at **reportphishing@apple.com**.)

- **Use Your Email's Reporting Tools** – Gmail, Outlook, and Yahoo all have "Report Phishing" buttons. Clicking it helps filter out scams for everyone.

- **Notify Authorities** – In the U.S., you can report scams to the **Federal Trade Commission (FTC)** at **reportfraud.ftc.gov**.

By reporting scams, you're **helping make the internet a safer place** for everyone.

Using Anti-Malware Tools to Stay Safe

Even if you're cautious, it's always good to have an **extra layer of protection**—like a security alarm for your MacBook. That's where **anti-malware software** comes in.

What is Anti-Malware Software?

Anti-malware (short for "anti-malicious software") helps detect and block harmful programs before they cause problems. It can catch viruses, spyware, and other sneaky threats **before** they affect your MacBook.

Which Anti-Malware Tools Should You Use?

There are plenty of security tools out there, but **stick to trusted names** like:

Malwarebytes – A great option for scanning and removing threats.
Norton 360 – A full security suite with automatic protection.
Apple's Built-In Security – macOS already has strong protections, so keeping it **updated** is key.

Best Practices for Staying Protected

- **Run Security Scans Regularly** – Set your anti-malware software to scan your MacBook on a schedule.

- **Keep Your Software Up to Date** – Updates **aren't just about new features**—they fix security holes, too!

- **Be Careful What You Download** – Only install apps from trusted sources, like the **Mac App Store or official company websites.**

With these tools in place, your MacBook will have **a strong defense** against online threats.

Celebrate Your Progress!

You've just learned some of the most important steps to **staying safe online**—from recognizing scams to reporting fraud and using security tools. Just like locking your doors at night, these habits will help protect your personal information so you can **browse with confidence.**

Security can feel overwhelming at first, but remember: **you don't have to know everything at once.** The more you practice safe browsing habits, the more natural they'll become. **You're doing a great job!**

If you ever feel unsure about an email, website, or download, **pause and ask for help.** Trust your instincts, take your time, and don't let scammers pressure you into quick decisions. **You've got this!**

Troubleshooting and Maintenance

DIGITAL GRANDSON PRESS

TROUBLESHOOTING COMMON MACBOOK PROBLEMS

SIMPLE FIXES TO KEEP YOUR MAC RUNNING SMOOTHLY

We've all been there—you're in the middle of something important, and suddenly your MacBook stops cooperating. Maybe the screen freezes, the Wi-Fi won't connect, or your Bluetooth device refuses to pair. It can be frustrating, but don't worry. Most common issues have simple solutions, and I'll walk you through them step by step.

The good news? Every time you troubleshoot a problem, you're building confidence and learning skills that make you more comfortable with your MacBook. Let's dive in and get you back on track.

Restart Your MacBook

Before anything else, let's try the fix that solves most tech problems—a good old-fashioned restart. Think of it like giving your MacBook a fresh start. It clears out digital clutter, resets connections, and often gets everything running smoothly again.

- **Restart from the Apple Menu** – If your MacBook is responding but sluggish, click the Apple icon in the top-left corner of your screen and select **Restart**. This is the easiest way to refresh your system.

- **Force Restart** – If your MacBook is completely frozen and unresponsive, press and hold the **power button** until the screen turns black. Wait a few seconds, then press the power button again to turn it back on.

- **When to Use Force Restart** – If you're in the middle of work and worried about losing progress, don't restart right away. Give your MacBook a moment to catch up—sometimes, it just needs an extra second. But if it's been frozen for more than a minute or two, a restart is your best option.

Restarting is a simple but powerful troubleshooting step. You'd be surprised how many times it fixes the problem on its own.

Fixing Wi-Fi and Bluetooth Issues

A stable internet connection is essential, whether you're browsing, emailing, or video calling family. And if your Bluetooth mouse, keyboard, or headphones won't connect, it can be just as frustrating. Let's go through the steps to get things working again.

Wi-Fi Troubleshooting

- **Check the Wi-Fi Icon** – Look at the **Wi-Fi icon** in the top-right corner of your screen. If it's grayed out, your Wi-Fi is off. Click the icon and select your home network.

- **Turn Wi-Fi Off and On** – Click the **Wi-Fi icon**, use the blue toggle switch to turn it off, wait a few seconds, and then turn it back on. This refreshes your connection.

- **Restart Your Router** – If your MacBook still won't connect, the issue may be with your internet provider or router. Unplug your router for **10**

seconds, then plug it back in. It may take a minute to fully reconnect.

- **Forget and Reconnect to Your Network** – If your Wi-Fi is connected but not working properly, try forgetting the network and reconnecting:

  a. Click the Apple menu and go to **System Settings** > **Wi-Fi**

  b. Select your network and click **Forget This Network**

  c. Reconnect by selecting your Wi-Fi and entering the password

Bluetooth Troubleshooting

- **Check Bluetooth Status** – Click the **Bluetooth icon** in the menu bar. If it's off, turn it back on.

- **Unpair and Re-Pair Devices** – If a Bluetooth device isn't working, try removing it and reconnecting:

  a. Click the **Bluetooth icon** and open **Bluetooth Settings**

  b. Find the device and click **Remove**

  c. Put the device into pairing mode and reconnect it

- **Restart Your MacBook** – If Bluetooth still isn't working, a restart may resolve the issue.

Wi-Fi and Bluetooth problems can be frustrating, but they're usually easy to fix with these simple steps.

When to Contact Apple Support

Sometimes, despite your best troubleshooting efforts, the problem persists. That's okay—knowing when to get professional help is just as important as knowing how to fix things yourself.

You should contact **Apple Support** if:

- Your **MacBook freezes frequently**, even after restarting

- The **screen flickers or shows strange colors**

- Your **battery won't charge or drains abnormally fast**

- You hear **strange noises from inside your MacBook**

To reach Apple Support, visit **support.apple.com** or open the **Apple Support app** on your iPhone or iPad. They can help you determine whether the issue requires repair or if there's another fix you can try.

Reaching out for help doesn't mean you've failed—it means you're taking charge of your technology.

Celebrate Your Troubleshooting Success

Look at you—solving tech problems like a pro! Every time you troubleshoot an issue, you're learning new skills and becoming more comfortable with your MacBook. The next time your Wi-Fi drops or an app freezes, you won't panic—you'll know exactly what to do.

And if all else fails, now you know how to reach out for help when you need it. That's a win!

Keep practicing, keep learning, and most importantly, **keep enjoying your MacBook**. You've got this!

GIVE YOUR MACBOOK A FRESH START: SIMPLE WAYS TO CLEAN UP AND SPEED UP

CLEAR THE CLUTTER, FREE UP SPACE, AND GET YOUR MACBOOK RUNNING LIKE NEW AGAIN!

Your MacBook is like a well-loved home—it holds everything you need, but over time, things pile up. Just like tidying up a cluttered closet or clearing off the kitchen counter, your MacBook needs a little maintenance now and then to keep it running smoothly. Whether you're running low on storage, noticing things feel a little sluggish, or just want a fresh start, this chapter will walk you through simple ways to clean up and speed up your MacBook. Let's dive in and give your Mac a refresh!

Check Your Storage Space

Before we start cleaning up, let's take a look at **what's actually taking up space**—because just like a closet, some things are worth keeping, and some things are just collecting dust.

1. **Check your storage usage** – Press **Command + Spacebar**, type **Storage**, and hit **Return**.

2. **See what's taking up space** – You'll see a colorful bar showing categories like "System," "Documents," "Photos," and "Other."

If your MacBook is nearly full, don't worry—there are **simple ways to free up space without deleting anything important.**

Clear Out Unnecessary Files and Apps

Now that you know what's filling up your storage, let's **declutter** by removing things you no longer need.

1. Empty the Trash Bin

Just like taking out the kitchen garbage, cleaning up your Mac starts with **emptying the Trash.**

- Click the **Trash** icon in the Dock.

- In the top-right corner, click **Empty**.

Until you do this, deleted files are **still taking up space** on your Mac—so consider this step your digital garbage day!

2. Delete Unused Apps

If you haven't used an app in months (or years), it's time to say goodbye.

- Open **Finder**, click **Applications**, and scroll through your apps.

- Right-click any app you don't use and select **Move to Trash**.

That random photo-editing app from 2015? Gone. The game you downloaded once and never played again? See ya.

3. Clear Out Old Downloads

Your **Downloads** folder is like that one drawer in the kitchen—full of random things you thought you might need but completely forgot about.

- Open **Finder**, click **Downloads**, and delete anything you don't need.

If you see old PDFs, duplicate photos, or outdated files, toss them out!

Speed Things Up for a Smoother Experience

If your MacBook has been feeling sluggish, there are a few easy ways to give it a little boost—kind of like a morning cup of coffee for your computer.

1. Close Unused Apps

- **Look at your Dock**—if an app has a dot under it, that means it's open.

- **Right-click** the app and select **Quit** if you're not using it.

Too many open apps can slow things down, just like having too many pots on the stove at once.

2. Manage Startup Apps

Some apps **automatically open** when you start your Mac, which can slow things down. Let's take control of that.

- Press **Command + Spacebar**, type **Login Items**, and hit **Return**.

- Look through the list and **toggle off** anything you don't need to start automatically.

This is like streamlining your morning routine—less clutter, less chaos, and a smoother start to your day.

Celebrate Your Clean MacBook

You did it! Your MacBook is now cleaner, faster, and more organized. Taking a few minutes to **declutter your files, remove old apps, and optimize your settings** can make a **huge** difference in how smoothly everything runs.

Just like keeping your home tidy, a little regular maintenance goes a long way. And the best part? Now you have **more space for the things that truly matter**—your photos, your favorite apps, and all the little things that make your Mac experience uniquely yours.

So go ahead—enjoy your refreshed MacBook. You've earned it!

GETTING HELP WHEN YOU NEED IT

REACHING OUT TO APPLE SUPPORT

Technology is amazing—until it isn't. We've all had those moments when our MacBook refuses to cooperate, and no amount of restarting or troubleshooting seems to fix the issue. When that happens, it's **not your fault**—sometimes, even the best technology needs a little professional help.

That's where **Apple Support** comes in. They've seen it all, from frozen screens to mysterious error messages. And the good news? **You're not alone in this.** Knowing when to reach out for help—and how to get the most out of the experience—can save you time, frustration, and even money.

Let's go over how to recognize when it's time to call in the experts, how to contact Apple Support, and how to make the process smooth and stress-free.

How to Know When It's Time to Ask for Help

Most minor MacBook issues can be fixed with a **restart** or a few quick adjustments. But sometimes, you'll run into a problem that's beyond DIY troubleshooting. Here are some signs that it's time to call in the pros:

- **Your MacBook keeps crashing or freezing** – If you've restarted, updated your software, and cleared some space, but your MacBook **still** locks up randomly, it could be a deeper issue. Think of it like a car that keeps stalling—time to get it checked out.

- **Something is physically broken** – If your screen flickers, the trackpad stops responding, or your keys don't register, these are likely hardware issues. Apple can diagnose whether it's a simple fix or something more serious.

- **Your battery isn't holding a charge** – If your MacBook dies quickly even when you're not using it, won't charge at all, or runs **hot** even when doing light tasks, it might need a battery checkup.

- **You keep seeing error messages you don't understand** – If you're getting pop-ups with cryptic warnings and Google isn't giving you a clear answer, Apple Support can help translate the tech jargon and guide you to a fix.

- **Wi-Fi or Bluetooth won't work no matter what you try** – If reconnecting, restarting, and resetting your network settings hasn't worked, it could be a deeper system issue.

- **You suspect a virus or malware** – While rare on a MacBook, if your system is running oddly slow, behaving unpredictably, or you're seeing weird ads or pop-ups, it's best to get expert advice.

If any of these sound familiar, don't worry—**you've already taken the first smart step by recognizing when to ask for help.**

The Best Ways to Contact Apple Support

Apple offers **several** ways to get help, depending on what works best for you. No long hold times, no confusing phone trees—just straightforward support.

1. Use the Apple Support Website

Go to **support.apple.com**. Here, you'll find articles, step-by-step guides, and troubleshooting tools. If you still need help, you can **schedule a call, start a chat, or book a repair.**

Think of this like checking the FAQ section before calling customer service—you might find the answer you need right away.

2. Use the Apple Support App

If you have an iPhone or iPad, download the **Apple Support app** from the App Store. This lets you message a support agent, schedule an appointment, or even run a diagnostic test on your MacBook.

It's like having a direct line to Apple's help desk—without waiting on hold.

3. Call Apple Support

If you prefer talking to a real person, call **1-800-APL-CARE (1-800-275-2273)** in the U.S. Apple's support team is known for being friendly, patient, and great at explaining things in simple terms.

It's like calling a tech-savvy friend—except this friend actually knows what they're talking about.

4. Visit the Apple Store (Genius Bar)

For hands-on help, you can make an appointment at your local **Apple Store Genius Bar**. They'll run tests on your MacBook and give you repair options if needed.

It's like taking your car to the mechanic—sometimes, an expert needs to see it in person.

How to Make Your Support Experience Smoother

To **save time** and get the best help possible, a little prep work goes a long way. Here's how to get the most out of your Apple Support experience:

- **Write down the problem before calling.** Jot down what's happening, when it started, and any steps you've already tried. The more details you provide, the quicker they can diagnose the issue.

- **Know your Apple ID and password.** Apple Support may need to verify your account, so have your login info handy.

- **Bring your charger if visiting the Apple Store.** Some issues, like battery problems, might be related to your charger, so bring it along just in case.

- **Stay calm and be specific.** The more clearly you can describe the issue, the faster they can help. If something doesn't make sense, ask them to explain it in simpler terms—they're happy to do so!

- **Take notes.** If Apple Support gives you troubleshooting steps, write them down in case the problem happens again.

You've Got This—And Help is Always Available

Asking for help is **not a sign of failure—it's a sign that you're being smart about solving the problem.** Even the most tech-savvy people rely on Apple Support from time to time.

By learning when to troubleshoot on your own and when to call in the experts, you're **taking control of your MacBook experience.** Each issue you tackle makes you more confident and capable, and that's something to be proud of.

So the next time your MacBook throws a tantrum, you'll know exactly what to do. And if you ever need a little extra help, **Apple Support is just a call or click away.** Keep up the great work!

Conclusion

DIGITAL GRANDSON PRESS

Celebrating Your Progress and Looking Ahead

You Did It! Now, Keep Going!

You made it! You've come a long way on this journey, and now it's time to pause, reflect, and celebrate your accomplishments. From setting up your MacBook to mastering shortcuts and syncing with other devices, you've built a strong foundation that will serve you well in your daily life.

Learning something new can feel like climbing a mountain, but step by step, you've reached the top. Remember how overwhelming it felt to take your MacBook out of the box for the first time? And now, here you are—navigating apps, managing files, connecting with family and friends, and even using Siri to make life easier. That's no small thing!

Let's take a moment to reflect on how far you've come, celebrate your wins, and look ahead to what's next.

Look at What You've Accomplished

Every challenge you've tackled has brought you closer to mastering your MacBook. Here are just a few of the skills you've learned:

- **Setting Up and Personalizing Your MacBook** – From creating an Apple ID to adjusting settings that make your MacBook more comfortable to use, you've made it feel like it's truly yours.

- **Organizing Files and Folders** – No more searching endlessly for documents. You've learned how to use Finder, create folders, and keep everything in its place.

- **Communicating with Ease** – Whether it's sending emails, using Messages, or hopping on a FaceTime call, you've figured out how to stay connected with the people who matter most.

- **Mastering Shortcuts and Siri** – What once seemed complicated—like using keyboard shortcuts or asking Siri for help—now feels like second nature.

- **Staying Secure Online** – You've learned how to create strong passwords, avoid scams, and keep your MacBook running smoothly and safely.

Each of these skills has given you more independence and confidence with technology. It's like learning to drive—what once felt overwhelming is now something you can do without even thinking about it.

Keep Exploring—You've Got This!

The great thing about technology is that there's always something new to learn. That might sound intimidating, but think of it as an opportunity. Every new feature you discover is another way to make your MacBook work better for you.

So, what's next? Maybe you'll:

- Create custom photo albums in the **Photos app** and share them with family.

- Experiment with editing a video or recording a voice memo.

- Use the **Notes app** to organize recipes, travel plans, or favorite quotes.

- Try out a new **app from the App Store** that makes your life easier or more fun.

Whatever you choose, **take it one step at a time.** You don't need to know everything all at once—just like you didn't learn to drive in a single day. The key is to stay curious and keep trying new things.

And if you ever get stuck? That's okay! Even the most tech-savvy people run into roadblocks. Remember, you've got plenty of ways to get help:

- **Revisit this guide**—there's no shame in going back over a chapter when you need a refresher.

- **Ask a trusted friend or family member**—they'd love to help, just like I've loved guiding you.

- **Look up a solution online**—you'd be surprised how many people have had the same question before you.

A Challenge for You

Now that you've come this far, I have a little challenge for you. Pick **one** thing on your MacBook that you haven't explored yet—maybe a new app, a setting you've never changed, or even just organizing your desktop. Give it a try. Click around. See what happens.

If you make a mistake? No big deal. Most things can be undone, and you can always ask for help. The important thing is that you keep learning, because every time you figure something out, you grow more confident.

You're Not Just Learning—You're Thriving

You're doing more than just learning how to use a computer—you're proving to yourself that you can take on new challenges, adapt to change, and stay connected in a digital world. That's something to be **proud of.** And I'm proud of you too.

So here's to you—to the progress you've made, the skills you've gained, and the adventures still ahead. Keep up the great work, keep exploring, and most of all, have fun along the way.

And remember—if you ever need a little tech help, just imagine your **digital grandson** sitting next to you, guiding you through it.

You've got this!

KEEP LEARNING: STAYING CONFIDENT WITH YOUR MACBOOK

HOW TO KEEP UP WITH CHANGES AND CONTINUE BUILDING YOUR SKILLS

You've come a long way on your MacBook journey, and I couldn't be prouder of you. But as you've probably noticed, technology doesn't stay the same for long. Updates bring new features, menus sometimes change, and every now and then, something that used to feel familiar suddenly looks different.

That's completely normal—and you don't have to keep up with everything all at once. The key is to stay curious, keep exploring, and know that help is always available when you need it. In this chapter, we'll go over ways to continue learning so you can feel confident with your MacBook, no matter what changes come your way.

Finding Easy-to-Follow Tutorials

One of the best ways to keep learning is to take advantage of online resources. Think of it like having a library that's always open, where you can look up exactly what you need, whenever you need it.

Visit The Digital Grandson's Guide to Tech

I built **The Digital Grandson's Guide to Tech** website just for you. It's a place where you can find easy-to-follow tutorials, updates on new features, and answers to common questions. I designed it to be simple, straightforward, and always there when you need a little extra help.

Go ahead and **bookmark it in your browser** so you can come back anytime. Think of it like keeping a favorite cookbook on the kitchen counter—whenever you need a refresher, it's right there waiting for you.

Try YouTube for Step-by-Step Videos

If you prefer to learn by watching, YouTube is a great place to find tutorials. Just type your question into the search bar, and you'll likely find a video walking you through it step by step.

The best part? You can **pause, rewind, or rewatch** as many times as you need—no need to worry about keeping up. It's like having a patient teacher who's happy to repeat themselves as many times as you want.

Joining MacBook Communities

Another great way to keep learning is to connect with others who are also using MacBooks. Sometimes, hearing how someone else solved a problem can help you figure things out faster.

Apple Support Communities

Apple has an official online forum where MacBook users ask and answer questions. You can browse discussions, see how others have solved similar issues, or even post a question yourself. It's like a neighborhood bulletin board where people share advice and help each other out.

Social Media Groups

There are also Facebook groups and online forums where people discuss Mac-Books and technology in general. These groups can be great for picking up tips, learning about new features, or just chatting with others who are also figuring things out.

And of course, don't forget about **friends and family**. If you know someone who's comfortable with technology, don't be shy about asking them questions. Most people are happy to share what they know, and sometimes, having someone explain it in person makes all the difference.

Keeping Up with macOS Updates

Every now and then, your MacBook will let you know that an update is available. These updates keep your computer running smoothly, fix security issues, and sometimes introduce new features.

If you see a message about an update, don't worry—it's nothing to be afraid of. Just click on it and follow the instructions. If you're unsure, you can check for updates manually:

- **Press Command + Spacebar** to open Spotlight Search

- Type **"Software Update"** and hit **Return**

- If an update is available, follow the on-screen steps

Sometimes updates will change how things look—maybe a button moves or a menu gets a new design. That's okay. Think of it like rearranging your kitchen cabinets: at first, you might reach for the plates and grab a bag of flour by mistake. But after a few days, you start to realize that the new setup actually makes more sense.

And remember, if something looks different after an update, you can always look it up, ask a friend, or check **The Digital Grandson's Guide to Tech** for help.

Celebrate Your Curiosity

The best thing you can do to keep learning is **stay curious**. Click on things, try new features, and don't be afraid to explore. Most of the time, if you make a mistake, it's **easily fixable**—and even when it's not, there's always a way to get back on track.

Technology is always changing, and that's okay. The important thing is that **you now know how to learn**. You've proven that you can figure things out, and that's a skill that will serve you well no matter what updates or changes come your way.

So keep that curiosity alive. Keep celebrating the small victories, whether it's learning a new shortcut or figuring out a new setting. Every step forward is progress, and you're doing an amazing job.

You've Got This!

You've come so far, and I couldn't be prouder. If you ever need a refresher, come back to this guide, visit **The Digital Grandson's Guide to Tech**, or reach out for help. You're never alone in this journey—there's always a way forward.

So keep exploring, keep learning, and most of all, **enjoy your MacBook**. You've got this!

The Digital Grandson's Tech Glossary

Simple Explanations and Helpful Tips for Navigating the Digital World with Confidence

Welcome to Your Tech Glossary!

Learning new technology can feel a bit like learning a new language, especially with so many unfamiliar words. But don't worry—you're not alone! This glossary is here to help. Whenever you come across a term you don't recognize, simply look it up here for a quick and friendly explanation. Think of it as your trusty guidebook, always ready to make your journey with technology a little easier. And remember, it's okay to take your time—learning is all about taking small steps forward. You've got this!

Activity Monitor: A tool on MacBooks that shows you what apps are running and how much energy they are using—great for troubleshooting.

AI (Artificial Intelligence): AI stands for Artificial Intelligence. It's the ability of a computer program to perform tasks that normally require human thinking—like answering questions, making suggestions, or understanding language.

AirDrop: A quick and easy way to share files between Apple devices without needing an internet connection, like sending a digital postcard.

Airplane Mode: A setting on your smartphone that turns off wireless connections like Wi-Fi, cellular, and Bluetooth. It's useful for saving battery or when you're on a plane.

Alexa: Amazon's voice-activated assistant, used in Echo devices. Alexa can help with tasks like playing music, setting reminders, providing weather updates, or controlling smart home gadgets—just by asking.

Amazon Appstore: An app store created by Amazon, similar to Google Play or Apple's App Store, where you can download apps for your devices.

Amazon Echo: A smart speaker created by Amazon, which uses Alexa to answer questions, play music, control smart home devices, and more.

Amazon Fire TV: A device that lets you stream movies, shows, and other content from the internet directly to your television.

Amazon Prime Video: A streaming service included with Amazon Prime. It offers movies, TV shows, and Amazon originals that you can watch online.

Amazon Prime: A subscription service that provides benefits like free shipping on many products, access to streaming movies and shows, and more. It's like getting VIP treatment for your shopping.

Amazon: An online shopping platform that started as a bookstore and quickly grew into one of the largest e-commerce sites in the world. You can buy almost anything on Amazon, and they'll ship it right to your door.

Antivirus Software: A program designed to protect your computer from harmful software (malware) that could steal your information or damage your device. It's like having a guard dog for your computer, keeping it safe from intruders.

App Store/Play Store: The marketplace on your smartphone where you can download new apps. The App Store is for iPhones, while the Google Play Store is for Android devices.

App: A software application that you can download to your smartphone or tablet. Apps are designed for specific purposes, like navigation (Google Maps), shopping (Amazon), or social networking (Facebook).

Apple ID: Your personal account used to access all Apple services, like the App Store, iCloud, and FaceTime. It's like your key to the Apple world.

Apple Maps: A GPS and navigation app developed by Apple, used to get directions and find places of interest.

Apple Music: A music streaming service available on MacBooks, allowing you to listen to millions of songs without needing to purchase each one.

Apple Pay: A digital wallet service that allows you to make payments using your Apple devices without needing physical credit or debit cards.

Apple Pencil: A stylus designed to work with iPads, allowing for precise drawing and writing, great for creative tasks or taking notes.

Apple Silicon: Apple's own processors used in newer MacBooks, providing better performance and battery life compared to older models.

Apple Store: The place where you can purchase Apple products, apps, and accessories, either online or in physical retail stores.

Apple Watch: A smartwatch that pairs with your iPhone, helping you track your health, receive notifications, and even make calls.

Apple: A technology company known for creating easy-to-use consumer electronics like iPhones, iPads, and Mac computers. Apple products are designed to make everyday tasks like communication, browsing, and entertainment simpler and more enjoyable.

AppleCare: An extended warranty program from Apple that provides additional support and repairs for your MacBook.

AutoSum: A quick button in Excel that adds up a list of numbers for you with one click.

Autosave: A feature in Microsoft Office that automatically saves your work every few seconds so you don't lose progress.

Bluetooth: A wireless technology used to connect devices over short distances, like connecting your phone to wireless headphones or a speaker.

Browser: A program used to access and navigate the internet, such as Google Chrome, Safari, or Firefox.

Buffering: When a video pauses while it's loading more data to play smoothly. It's a bit like waiting for the rest of a page in a book to be printed while you're reading it.

Cache: A storage location on your device that keeps data from websites and apps to help them load faster next time you use them.

Canvas (ChatGPT Canvas): Canvas is a visual tool in ChatGPT that lets you organize thoughts like sticky notes on a digital board. You can move, label, and group your ideas to help plan or brainstorm.

Cart: A virtual shopping cart where you add items you want to buy while browsing an online store. It's just like using a cart in a physical store to hold all your items before you check out.

Chart (Column/Line/Pie): A visual way to show numbers in Excel using bars, lines, or pie slices instead of rows of data.

Chat (Conversation): A chat is the back-and-forth conversation you have with ChatGPT. You type something, it replies—and you can keep going as long as you like.

ChatGPT: ChatGPT is a friendly AI assistant made by OpenAI. You can ask it questions, get help writing or organizing things, and even have a casual conversation—just by typing or speaking.

Chat History: Chat History is a list of your past conversations with ChatGPT. You can go back to them, rename them, or delete them. If you turn chat history off, those chats won't be saved after 30 days.

Checkout: The process of reviewing your selected items, entering your payment information, and completing your purchase. Think of it like getting in line at a store's register—just online.

Clipboard (Copy, Cut, Paste): A short-term "holding tray" on your computer where copied or cut items wait until you paste them somewhere else.

Cloud Storage: A way to save data and files on remote servers that you can access from any device with an internet connection.

Command Key: A key on the MacBook keyboard used in combination with others to perform shortcuts, similar to the Control key on Windows.

Comment: A response to a post or photo that you can type out. It allows you to share your thoughts or interact with the content.

Confirmation Email: An email sent to you after making an online purchase, which includes the details of your order and confirmation that it was received.

Copilot (Microsoft Office): An AI helper built into Office programs that suggests drafts, summaries, or lists based on what you ask it to do.

Cortana: Cortana is Microsoft's voice-activated assistant, created to help you perform tasks, set reminders, and get answers to questions—just by speaking.

You can think of Cortana as your digital helper, designed to make using your computer a bit easier and more fun.

Custom GPT: A Custom GPT is a special version of ChatGPT created for a specific task, like teaching knitting or helping with recipes. You can find ones made by others or make your own with a few simple instructions.

DALL·E: DALL·E is a tool built into ChatGPT that turns words into pictures. Just describe what you want to see—like "a cat wearing sunglasses"—and it draws it. You can also edit parts of the image afterward.

Deep Research: Deep Research is a powerful feature in ChatGPT that works like an AI research assistant. It can search the web, read articles, compare information, and write a full report with sources. It's ideal for things like comparing products, exploring news, or learning about complex topics. Results take 5 to 30 minutes and are only available with certain plans.

Desktop: A computer that is designed to stay in one place, often found on desks. It usually has a separate monitor, keyboard, and mouse, and is great for working at home.

Device: An electronic tool like a smartphone, tablet, or computer that helps you interact with digital content.

Digital: Refers to anything involving computers, electronics, or the internet. It's like the difference between a paper photo and a picture on your phone—the digital version is the one you see on your screen.

Direct Message (DM): A private message you can send to someone on social media. Unlike comments, DMs are just between you and the person you're messaging.

Do Not Disturb: A setting on MacBooks that silences notifications so you can focus on work or relax without interruptions.

Dock: The bar at the bottom of the MacBook screen that shows your favorite apps for easy access, similar to a quick launch bar.

Download: The process of transferring data or software from the internet to your device.

Excel: A Microsoft Office program for organizing information in rows and columns, doing math, and spotting patterns.

FaceTime: An app on MacBooks that lets you make video calls to friends and family who also use Apple devices. It's like having a video chat built right in.

File: A collection of data stored on your computer, like a document or a photo. Think of it as a digital folder that holds information you need.

Finder Tags: Labels you can add to files and folders on your MacBook to make it easier to organize and search for documents.

Finder: A feature on MacBooks that helps you locate files, folders, and apps. It's like the file manager for all your documents.

Fingerprint Recognition: A security feature that uses your fingerprint to unlock a device or authorize a transaction.

Folder: A way to organize multiple files, similar to how you'd use a physical folder to keep papers together. It helps keep your computer neat and tidy.

Follower: Someone who subscribes to your social media account to see your posts and updates. It's like having a group of friends who want to stay in touch with what you're sharing.

Force Quit: A way to close an app that's not responding on your MacBook, similar to ending a task on a PC. It helps when an app gets stuck.

Gmail: An email service created by Google, which lets you send and receive messages. It's one of the most popular email platforms in the world.

Google Assistant: A voice-activated assistant by Google that helps you perform tasks, answer questions, and control smart home devices with simple voice commands.

Google Chrome: A web browser developed by Google that lets you explore the internet. It's known for being fast and easy to use.

Google Drive: A cloud storage service that allows you to store, share, and access your files from any device with an internet connection.

Google Maps: A navigation app that provides directions for driving, walking, cycling, and public transportation. It also helps you find local businesses and points of interest.

Google Photos: A photo storage service that automatically backs up your pictures and videos, making them easy to find and share.

Google: A technology company best known for its search engine, which helps you find information on the internet. Google also creates other helpful products and services.

GPS (Global Positioning System): A satellite-based navigation system that helps determine your exact location and provides directions to your destination.

GPT (Generative Pre-trained Transformer): GPT stands for Generative Pre-trained Transformer. It's the type of AI that powers ChatGPT. It "learns" from lots of reading and uses that knowledge to generate helpful answers.

GPT-4 / GPT-4o / GPT-3.5: These are different versions of the ChatGPT brain. GPT-3.5 is fast and free. GPT-4 is more advanced and accurate. GPT-4o is the newest version—it's even faster, better at understanding voice, and handles more complex tasks.

Handoff: A feature that lets you start a task on one Apple device, like writing an email, and continue it on another, such as your MacBook.

Hard Drive: The main storage device in your computer where all your files, apps, and data are stored. It's like the brain of your computer that remembers everything.

Home Button: A button found on many smartphones that takes you back to the main screen, just like the 'home' key on an old phone.

Hub: A device that serves as a central control point for other smart devices. A smart speaker, like Amazon Echo, can act as a hub for your smart home.

Hulu: A streaming service that offers TV shows, movies, and live television. It's great for catching up on episodes of your favorite shows.

iCloud: Apple's cloud storage service that helps you save photos, files, and other data online so you can access it from any of your devices.

Install: The process of adding an app or program to your device so you can use it.

Internet Connection: The service that allows your device to connect to the web, enabling you to browse websites, use apps, and communicate online.

Internet: The internet is like a giant web that connects computers all around the world. It allows you to access information, watch videos, send emails, and connect with people, no matter where they are.

iPad: A tablet developed by Apple, used for activities like browsing the internet, watching videos, and reading.

iPhone: A smartphone by Apple that combines calling, texting, apps, and internet browsing in one device.

Keychain: A password manager built into macOS that helps you store and manage your passwords securely, making it easier to log in to websites.

Kindle: Amazon's e-reader device that lets you download and read books electronically. It's like carrying an entire library in your bag without the weight.

Laptop: A portable computer that you can take with you. It's like having a desktop that you can carry around and use anywhere—perfect for when you want flexibility.

Launchpad: A feature that shows all of your installed apps in one place, similar to a home screen on a smartphone, for easy access.

Like: On social media platforms, a 'Like' is a way to show that you appreciate a post, photo, or video. It's a simple way to give a virtual thumbs-up.

MacBook Air: A lighter, more portable MacBook, great for everyday tasks like browsing the web, emailing, and streaming.

MacBook Pro: A more powerful version of the MacBook, often used for professional work like graphic design, video editing, or programming.

MacBook: A laptop computer made by Apple. It combines sleek design with user-friendly features, making it great for both work and play.

macOS: The operating system used by Mac computers, similar to how Windows works on PCs. It's what makes your MacBook run smoothly.

Magic Keyboard: Apple's wireless keyboard, known for its comfortable typing experience and compatibility with MacBooks.

Magic Mouse: A wireless mouse made by Apple that works with MacBooks, featuring a smooth, multi-touch surface for gestures.

MagSafe: A special power connector used by some MacBooks. It easily snaps into place and releases if pulled, preventing accidents.

Malware: Malware is harmful software that can sneak onto your device and cause trouble, like stealing information or slowing things down. It's kind of like those pesky weeds in a garden—they're unwanted and can be a real nuisance. Antivirus software helps keep malware away and protects your device.

Microsoft Office 365: A subscription service that provides access to Microsoft's main programs (Word, Excel, PowerPoint, Outlook) plus updates and cloud storage.

Microsoft Word (Word): A Microsoft Office program for creating documents, like a digital typewriter with tools for formatting and adding pictures.

Mission Control: A feature on MacBooks that shows all open windows and apps, making it easier to switch between tasks.

Navigation: The act of planning and following a route to get from one place to another, often using a GPS device or app.

Netflix: A popular streaming service that allows you to watch a variety of TV shows, movies, and documentaries. Think of it like a giant library of entertainment, available anytime you want.

Notification Bar: A section at the top of your smartphone screen that shows updates, messages, and alerts from your apps.

Notification: A pop-up alert on your device that informs you about updates, messages, or reminders from your apps.

Offline Maps: Maps that you can download to your device and use without an internet connection.

OneDrive: Microsoft's cloud storage service that saves your files online so you can access them from any device.

Online Shopping: Purchasing items from a website or app without having to visit a physical store. Products are delivered to your doorstep.

OpenAI: OpenAI is the company that created ChatGPT. They build tools that use artificial intelligence to help people learn, write, and solve problems.

Operating System: The software that runs your computer and allows all the other programs to work. Common ones are Windows for PCs and macOS for Apple computers—think of it as the boss that tells the computer how to do its job.

Outlook: A Microsoft Office program for email and calendars, helping you send messages and manage your schedule.

Passcode: A series of numbers or a pattern that you use to unlock your smartphone. It's like a digital key to keep your information safe.

Payment Method: The way you choose to pay for a purchase, such as using a credit card, debit card, or digital wallet.

Personalize: Customizing settings to fit your preferences, such as adjusting the volume of your smart speaker or selecting your favorite music service.

Personalized GPT: A Personalized GPT is one that's been trained to understand your preferences—like your name, favorite tone, or writing style—so it can respond in a more personal and helpful way.

Playlist: A collection of songs or videos that you can create and play in order. It's like making your own personalized mixtape, but for digital content.

PowerPoint: A Microsoft Office program for making slideshows with text, images, and charts.

Preview: An app on MacBooks that allows you to view and edit PDFs and images without needing additional software.

Project (ChatGPT Projects): A Project is a space where you can group related chats, files, and notes. It helps you stay organized when you're working on something bigger—like planning a trip or writing a story.

Prompt: A prompt is what you type into ChatGPT to get it started. It can be a question, a request, or a simple idea. Think of it like a conversation starter for your digital helper.

QR Code: A square barcode that can be scanned with your device's camera to open a website, download an app, or access information.

Reboot: Turning your computer off and back on again to help solve problems or apply updates. It's like giving your computer a fresh start.

Recovery Mode: A special startup mode for troubleshooting your MacBook, used to reinstall macOS or fix system issues.

Reminder: A notification set through your smart speaker or app to help you remember tasks, such as watering the plants or taking medication.

Retina Display: A type of high-resolution screen used in MacBooks that makes text and images look incredibly sharp and clear, almost like looking at a printed photo.

Return Policy: The rules set by an online store about returning purchased items. It tells you how long you have to return something, what items are eligible, and whether you'll get a refund or store credit.

Router: A device that connects your devices to the internet and allows them to communicate with each other wirelessly.

Safari: The default web browser on MacBooks. It's where you go to browse the internet, similar to Google Chrome or Firefox.

Satellite: A device in space that sends signals to GPS devices on Earth, helping determine your location.

Screen Timeout: A setting that controls how long your device stays on without activity before the screen turns off to save battery.

Search (Web Search in ChatGPT): Search is a feature that lets ChatGPT look things up on the internet in real time. It gives you quick answers from trusted websites—great for current events, live data, or anything not in its memory.

Shipping Address: The address where you want your purchased items delivered. It's important to double-check this so your package ends up at the right doorstep!

Sidecar: A feature that lets you use an iPad as a second screen for your MacBook, adding more screen space for multitasking.

Siri: Siri is Apple's voice-activated assistant, designed to help you do things like send messages, set reminders, or get answers to questions—just by asking. Siri can be found on Apple devices like iPhones, iPads, and the Apple Watch. Think of Siri as your helpful, virtual personal assistant.

Smart Home: A home equipped with smart devices, like speakers, lights, and thermostats, that can be controlled remotely using a smartphone or voice commands.

Smart Speaker: A voice-activated speaker that can play music, answer questions, control smart home devices, and more. Examples include Amazon Echo and Google Home.

Spotlight: A built-in search tool on MacBooks that helps you quickly find apps, documents, and other information. It's like having a super-fast digital assistant.

Streaming Service: A platform that lets you watch movies, TV shows, or listen to music online without needing to download anything. Examples include Netflix, Amazon Prime Video, Hulu, and Spotify.

Streaming: Watching or listening to content (like TV shows, music, or movies) directly from the internet without needing to download it.

Subscription: A recurring payment that gives you access to a service, like Netflix or Hulu. It's like joining a club where you pay a monthly fee to enjoy the content.

System Preferences: The settings area on your MacBook where you can adjust things like display, sound, and internet connections.

Tag: Mentioning someone in a post or photo by using the '@' symbol followed by their name. It's like giving someone a shout out to get their attention.

Taskbar: A bar that appears on your screen (usually at the bottom) that helps you switch between different programs and see what's open. Think of it like the remote control for your computer.

Thunderbolt Port: A high-speed connection port on MacBooks used for connecting accessories like external monitors or hard drives.

Time Machine: A backup feature on MacBooks that helps you create backups of your files, so you don't lose important data if something goes wrong.

Touch Bar: A strip of touch-sensitive buttons on some MacBook Pros that change based on the app you're using, providing quick shortcuts.

Touch ID: A fingerprint sensor on some MacBooks that allows you to unlock your device or make purchases securely with just a touch.

Touchscreen: The screen on your smartphone that responds to your touch. It's how you interact with apps, type messages, and navigate your device.

Tracking Number: A number provided by the shipping company that lets you track where your package is during delivery. It's like having a little map that shows your package's journey to your door.

Trackpad: The flat, touch-sensitive surface below the keyboard on a MacBook that you use to move the cursor and click, like a mouse.

Turn-By-Turn Directions: Step-by-step navigation instructions provided by GPS apps, guiding you on how to get to your destination.

Update: Installing the latest version of an app or software to get new features or fix problems.

USB Cable: A type of cable used to connect devices for charging or transferring data.

Voice Command: A spoken instruction that your smart speaker or GPS app can understand and respond to, such as "Play music" or "Get directions to the nearest gas station."

Wallpaper: The background image on your computer's desktop. You can personalize it with a photo of your choice, just like hanging a favorite picture in your room.

Waze: A GPS app known for providing real-time traffic updates, based on information shared by other drivers.

Website: A website is like a digital home on the internet where you can find information, shop, watch videos, or connect with others. Think of it like a library or store, but online.

Wi-Fi: A technology that allows devices to connect to the internet wirelessly. Wi-Fi is needed for most smart home devices and online activities.

Window: A framed area on your computer screen where a program is displayed. Just like a real window lets you see outside, a digital window lets you see different parts of a program.

Zoom: A feature that allows you to enlarge or shrink a view on your screen, useful when you need to see map details more clearly. It is also a video conferencing app.

Closing Note

This glossary is your handy tech companion. Keep it close by, and don't hesitate to refer to it whenever you need a little extra help. Remember, learning something new is all about taking one step at a time—and you're doing an amazing job. If you ever need more explanations or want extra tips, just visit www.thed igitalgrandson.com. I'm always here to help, like a tech-savvy grandchild who's just a click away!

—The Digital Grandson

About The Digital Grandson's Guide to Tech

Simple. Supportive. Made Just for You

You've just taken a big step into the digital world, and I hope it felt less like a chore and more like a cozy chat over coffee with someone who cares. That's what *The Digital Grandson's Guide to Tech* is all about: **Simple explanations. Kind encouragement. No eye-rolling.**

What We're Here For:

Clear, step-by-step tutorials
   No tech jargon. No "just Google it." Just plain-English guides to help you do

the things you want to do—whether that's sharing a photo, joining a video call, or shopping safely online.

Friendly, easy-to-use guidebooks

Like this one—built to sit proudly on your shelf and be flipped through anytime you need a refresher or a little boost of confidence.

Tip:

If you ever feel stuck, tired, or like you're the only one still figuring it out—**you're not.**

Take a break. Come back later. Ask for help.

This isn't a race—it's a journey, and you're doing beautifully.

Stay Curious. Stay Connected. Stay You.

Whether you keep learning with us online, pass this book along to a friend, or just take one new skill and run with it, know this:

You belong in the digital world.

And there's always a seat at our table for you.

With patience, care, and all the tech support you need,
—The Digital Grandson

ALSO BY THE DIGITAL GRANDSON'S GUIDE TO TECH

If you found this book helpful, you may like my other guides designed with the same clear, step-by-step approach. I wrote each one to take the mystery out of technology and make it feel simple, useful, and even a little fun.

You can find them all on Amazon—just search for *The Digital Grandson*.

THE ULTIMATE TECH BOOK FOR BEGINNERS AND SENIORS

- Whether you're new to computers, smartphones, or tablets, this guide walks you through the basics—step by step.
- No confusing terms, no pressure—just patient, large-print instructions you can follow at your own pace.

THE SOCIAL MEDIA BOOK FOR SENIORS

- This easy, large-print guide shows you how to use Facebook, Instagram, YouTube, and more—step by step.
- No tech jargon. Just clear, supportive help to connect with family, share photos, and stay safe online.
- Perfect for seniors, caregivers, and anyone new to social media.

THE COMPLETE MACBOOK FOR SENIORS GUIDE

- Whether you're using a MacBook Air or MacBook Pro, this beginner-friendly guide walks you through everything step by step—at your pace and in plain English.
- From turning it on to browsing the web, you'll get clear, large-print instructions with no confusion.

THE CHATGPT BOOK FOR BEGINNERS

- If you're curious about AI or just want a clear, practical way to start, this book walks you through step by step.
- Full of real-life examples, it helps you write better prompts, use AI tools confidently, and explore what ChatGPT can do —for work, learning, planning, and play.

THE ESSENTIAL IPHONE & IPAD GUIDE FOR SENIORS

- Learning your iPhone or iPad doesn't have to feel overwhelming.
- This friendly guide was written with you in mind—no jargon, no pressure, just clear, simple steps.

THE ESSENTIAL ONLINE SAFETY GUIDE FOR SENIORS

- You don't have to be tech-savvy to stay safe online.
- This friendly guide cuts through the noise and gives you simple, proven habits to protect passwords, spot scams, safeguard privacy, and recover if something goes wrong.

THE ESSENTIAL GUIDE TO EMAIL FOR SENIORS

- Tired of feeling lost in your inbox?
- This easy, large-print book shows you how to send, receive, and protect your email with confidence.

THE COMPLETE MICROSOFT OFFICE 365 GUIDE FOR BEGINNERS

- A clear, step-by-step manual for Word, Excel, PowerPoint, Outlook, and OneDrive.
- With simple instructions, practical examples, and time-saving habits, this Microsoft Office guide makes everyday tasks easy.

Take a moment to leave us a review!

If this book helped you feel more confident with email, I'd be grateful if you'd take a moment to go back and leave a brief review on Amazon!

Your feedback does two helpful things:

- It helps me keep improving future editions.

- It helps other readers — people who may be feeling just as unsure as you once did — discover that they're not alone and that learning email can be simple.

Even a single sentence makes a big impact.

Thank you for being part of this journey and for sharing your voice!

www.ingramcontent.com/pod-product-compliance
Lightning Source LLC
LaVergne TN
LVHW081527050326
832903LV00025B/1657